"Get ready to improve your l⸝ Dave and Jan Stoop give all ⸝ ⸝arning how to love SMART. Foll⸝ ⸝dance and your love life will never be the s

Drs. Les and Leslie Parrott, *New York Times* bestselling
authors of *Saving Your Marriage Before It Starts*

"Great marriages are both art and science. Dave and Jan Stoop have integrated both in a highly effective system, using the latest neuroscience, to bring couples more intimacy and happiness. Great concepts and very workable skills. I highly recommend this book."

John Townsend, PhD, *New York Times* bestselling author
of *Boundaries*; founder of the Townsend Institute
of Leadership and Counseling

"In the forest of books on marriage relationships, *The Emotionally Healthy Marriage* stands tall. Thanks to their years of professional practice, their knowledge of the Bible, the results of recent research on emotional intelligence, and their own vibrant marriage relationship, Dave and Jan have given us a unique and practical resource. The many Action Plans alone are worth the price of the book. No pie-in-the-sky platitudes or superficial solutions, but wise counsel that can make an immediate difference in your marriage."

Gary J. Oliver, ThM, PhD, executive director of the Center for
Healthy Relationships; professor of psychology and practical
theology at John Brown University; coauthor of *Mad About Us*

THE
EMOTIONALLY
HEALTHY
MARRIAGE

Books by David and Jan Stoop

Just Us

The Emotionally Healthy Marriage

Books by David Stoop

Making Peace with Your Father

You Are What You Think

Forgiving Our Parents, Forgiving Ourselves

Rethink How You Think

Forgiving What You'll Never Forget

THE
EMOTIONALLY
HEALTHY
MARRIAGE

*GROWING CLOSER BY
UNDERSTANDING EACH OTHER*

DR. DAVID STOOP & DR. JAN STOOP

Revell
a division of Baker Publishing Group
Grand Rapids, Michigan

Published by Revell
a division of Baker Publishing Group
PO Box 6287, Grand Rapids, MI 49516-6287
www.revellbooks.com

Repackaged edition published 2020
ISBN 978-0-8007-3832-7

Previously published in 2017 under the title *SMART Love*

Printed in the United States of America

The Library of Congress has cataloged the original edition as follows:
Names: Stoop, David A., author.
Title: SMART love : how improving your emotional intelligence will transform your
    marriage / Dr. David Stoop and Dr. Jan Stoop.
Description: Grand Rapids : Revell, 2017. | Includes bibliographical references.
Identifiers: LCCN 2016039043 | ISBN 9780800727550 (pbk.)
Subjects: LCSH: Marriage—Religious aspects—Christianity. | Emotional
    intelligence. | Emotions—Religious aspects—Christianity.
Classification: LCC BV835 .S7773 2017 | DDC 248.8/44—dc23
LC record available at https://lccn.loc.gov/2016039043

This publication is intended to provide helpful and informative material on the subjects addressed. Readers should consult their personal health professionals before adopting any of the suggestions in this book or drawing inferences from it. The authors and publisher expressly disclaim responsibility for any adverse effects arising from the use or application of the information contained in this book.

The names and details of the people and situations described in this book have been changed or presented in composite form in order to ensure the privacy of those with whom the authors have worked.

The authors are represented by WordServe Literary Group (www.wordserveliterary .com).

Baker Publishing Group publications use paper produced from sustainable forestry practices and post-consumer waste whenever possible.

CONTENTS

INTRODUCTION

In 1995, Daniel Goleman published his book titled *Emotional Intelligence*, in which he defined five skills that represented the concept of emotional intelligence, or what we refer to as *EQ*: (1) self-awareness, (2) self-regulation, (3) motivation, (4) empathy, and (5) social skills. Although he included romantic relationships and family relationships in his book, his ideas quickly captured the business world.

Over the years since, researchers have found that EQ was the single most important quality that defines someone as a truly effective leader. It is more important than cognitive intelligence, leadership skills, or even experience. They found that 90 percent of high performers in business understood and practiced EQ. The link between emotional intelligence and what a person earns is so direct that with every point increase on a person's EQ score, their annual salary increased by $1,300.

Eventually the five skills of EQ were reduced to four. The skills are now called competencies, and they are (1) self-awareness, (2) self-management, (3) social awareness, and

(4) relationship management. They form the foundation of what we call SMART Love as we relate the principles primarily to marriage. There is no connection between IQ and EQ. A person may have an IQ of 140 but be totally ineffective when it comes to EQ because they have never developed the necessary skills to navigate the world of emotions.

As of this writing, over half a million people have been tested for EQ, and researchers have found that only 36 percent of the people tested were able to identify their emotions as they happened,[1] which is the foundational skill of both EQ and SMART Love. Without the skills of SMART Love, a person not only will be less effective in business but will have a hard time effectively relating to the primary people in their personal life.

The more we have studied EQ and how powerful it is in the business world, the more we see the connection it has to all of our relationships. It affects our parenting, our friendships, and especially our marriages. It gives us insight into how important understanding emotion is and how learning to manage our emotions can make every relationship stronger. That's why we call it SMART Love.

Note: When we use "I" in the book, it refers to Dave, as he is the one in clinical practice.

What Is SMART Love?

In successful, satisfying marriages, couples have learned how to be comfortable together in the land of emotions. They have learned to do the "not easy" part of what Aristotle once described: "Anyone can become angry—that is easy. But to be angry with the right person, to the right degree, at the right time, for the right purpose, and in the right way, that is not easy."[1] Couples who have learned how to navigate the complex world of emotions experience what we call *SMART Love*.

SMART Love is based on the principles of emotional intelligence (EQ), which have been developed primarily within the business world. Emotions and how we manage them play an important role in the business world, but the skills of emotional intelligence are even more important in our personal relationships, in our family, and especially in our marriage. The difference between a so-so marriage and a great marriage comes down to how "SMART" we are about love. It's not just about how many workshops we've attended as a couple. It's not about how many marital counseling sessions we've experienced together. It's not about what conflict resolution skills we've been taught, or even based on how much we know about how relationships work in general. And it's not based on our ability to carry on a conversation together, although that may be part of it. It's about knowing how to develop, express, and experience the skills of SMART Love.

SMART is an acronym for the five competencies of SMART Love. You can experience SMART Love when the following are present in your life:

Self-awareness of your emotions.

Managing your emotions.

Accountability to yourself, your spouse, and others.

Reading the other person's emotions.

Together in the land of emotions.

The problems encountered in our learning how to love SMART are not limited to one gender, even though it might seem so. It's true that men are often like strangers in the land of emotions, many of them not even able to come up with the words to describe their emotions. While women aren't afraid to talk about emotions, they do this primarily with their female friends. When it comes to talking about their emotions with their husbands, they may also be at a loss for how to do it successfully.

As humans, we are emotional beings. We are all created in the image of God, and that includes being emotional. After all, the God of the Bible is an emotional God. In 1 John 4,

John tells us that the very essence of God is love. To truly know him is to experience his love. In fact, not only is God the personification of love, but "love comes from God" (v. 7). The Bible, mostly in the Old Testament, also describes God as feeling anger. He is angry about sin, and he was angry at his people, Israel, who were so rejecting of his love and so sinful. To solve the sin problem, and because he is righteous and loves us so much, he sent his Son to die in our place to bear the punishment for our sins.

God also experiences sadness. In Hosea, God says, "Oh, how can I give you up, Israel? How can I let you go? . . . My heart is torn within me, and my compassion overflows" (Hos. 11:8). That's an emotional passage!

God feels joy as well. We are told there is great joy in heaven when a sinner repents (see Luke 15:7). Since we are emotional creatures created in God's image, it's important to better understand the emotions we all experience so we can become comfortable in the land of emotions.

Of course, not all emotions are positive. For example, we've all been there, at least to some degree, when what starts out as an innocent conversation suddenly hits a trigger point, and before either of us knows what's happening, we're in the middle of a highly emotional argument. Passion suddenly overwhelms all sense of reason. Quickly, one or both of us gets out of control, saying things we're going to regret later when we calm down. Sometimes the arguments can become so emotional that neither one of us can even remember what started it. One—or more likely both—of us has just had our reasoning hijacked by our emotions.

As we teach couples about SMART Love, they find it is a fresh vantage point from which they can view their own and their spouse's emotional reactions. They each can learn how to be intentionally SMART about their emotions.

Fear and Anger

As a counselor, I hear stories over and over that are similar to the experience of Pat and Don. As they sat in my office, they told me about what they called their out-of-control arguments. As we started the first session, it quickly became obvious what they were talking about. They had plenty of emotions in their marriage, but they hadn't yet learned how to manage them. Even though they were both able to express their emotions, they were strangers in the world of SMART Love. Here's what happened in their first session.

When I asked what brought them to counseling, they looked at each other for a moment and then Pat jumped in. She said she was wrapping her mother's birthday gift and had hoped to have it done before Don came home. She knew the sight of the gift would kick off a violent argument, but she had gotten busy doing some other things, and then it was too late. Don walked into the kitchen just as she was finishing wrapping.

She said he demanded to know what she was working on as he asked, "What's that you're wrapping?"

Don started to jump in to defend himself, but I motioned for him to wait. I reassured him he would get his turn.

Pat continued. "I told him it was just something for my mom's birthday. He pretended to be interested, asking sarcastically what I got her. He will deny the sarcasm, but we've been down this road about my mother so many times I don't remember how I responded—I probably wasn't nice. I think

I said something like, 'What difference does it make to you?' He pressed, so I finally said it was my mom's sixty-fifth birthday and I got her a gold bracelet. I knew the minute I said 'gold' I should have kept my mouth shut. He yelled at me something like, 'Gold? Like 14k? How much did you spend this time?'"

Pat said she didn't remember what happened after that. Don just exploded, and she exploded back. She added, "I know I said things I'm sorry for now, especially because the children heard some of the hurtful things we both said. We've got to break the cycle—I can't stand living like this!"

I then turned to Don and asked, "How do you see what happened?"

He was quiet for a while, and then he quickly ramped up as he started to describe what he thought was the real problem. "It's her mother—that's the issue for me." He went on to describe what he saw as unfairness in how Pat favored her mother and bought her all kinds of things. He said she didn't need a birthday as an excuse to surprise her mother with some gift. She talked with her mother every day, and he was convinced she didn't really like *his* mother.

They had been married for nineteen years, but the mother-in-law issue was still alive and well. Pat jumped in and added that his mother still treated him like a boy, not a man. And Don just as quickly threw back at her that at least his mother respected him, which was more than Pat did.

"How do the arguments end?" I asked.

Pat answered, "I typically storm out of the room and we don't talk for days."

"This time, when we started talking again, we both realized we needed some help to break the cycle," Don added.

Pat and Don were involved in two battles. The obvious problem in their argument was the issue of the perceived unfairness about the amount of money Pat spent on the two mothers. But the real problem was what was going on in the two different parts of their brains. You could say that God designed our brains to have an emotional center and a rational center. For both Pat and Don, their emotions were engaged in battle with their reason, and the emotional brain seemed to win most often. Couples experiencing that internal battle between their two brains, like Don and Pat were, find that the emotional brain usually wins the battle. The rational brain is ignored by their emotional brain.

It seems so natural, the dominance of our emotions. And it *is* natural. Whenever we see or hear something, it enters our brain and goes immediately to our limbic system, which is the emotional center of our brain. A key part of our limbic system—the amygdala—sounds the alarm that some new information is coming in and goes on alert to identify any potential danger. The amygdala's primary orientation is fear, and that's for a reason—to protect us from anything that threatens us. Don felt threatened. And his fear said to him, "Oh no, this spending is out of control again! We can't allow that to happen!"

Pat's emotional system was also on the lookout and was already prepared for the worst. Her emotional brain bypassed her rational brain as well, and when the conversation exploded, she was just as out of control as Don. For both Don and Pat, the information was never sent to the rational control center of the brain. The emotional part of the brain wouldn't forward the message. It had blocked out the reasoning part. Maybe later, when things calmed down, their brains would deal with the situation rationally, but by then it would be too late—the hurt and damage were already done.

Sometimes the lack of SMART Love results in not being able to enjoy something someone else is enjoying. Angie's mom and dad are like that. They are the opposite of Don and Pat. They never argue. If you were to watch them interact, you might wonder if they experienced any emotions at all.

Angie is in the tenth grade and is typically a B student. But as she started her classes in the fall, she determined to do better. She decided she wanted to get into a good college after high school and realized how important her grades would be in determining what college she would attend. So she worked hard on her homework and asked for extra help in a couple of classes, and at the end of the first semester her final grades were four A's and two B's. She was ecstatic—she radiated great joy at her success, and she couldn't wait to show her grades to her parents. But when she did, all they said in response was, "That's nice." And with that, her dad picked up the newspaper to continue his reading, and her mom turned back to the TV program she had been watching.

Angie was crushed by her parents' lack of response, but as she thought about it, she wasn't surprised. Neither of her parents ever showed any emotion. If it weren't for Angie and her siblings, their house would be an emotional wasteland. She lived with two parents who were terrified to enter the land of emotions, even when it came to their daughter, who desperately needed to be affirmed.

To say that Angie's parents expressed no emotion is probably not accurate, for they were dominated by one of the negative emotions—fear. Something had to have happened as they were growing up that made the experience of any emotion scary and a thing to be avoided. They experienced an overwhelming amount of fear, even as they related to their children.

Sometimes only one person in the marital relationship seems to show any emotions. Kimberly told me that she was the one in her marriage who was the hothead. Every time there was a potential argument, she was the one who would lose control emotionally. Jerry might lose his temper and explode back at Kimberly as she railed at him, but only on rare occasions and when she didn't let up with the accusations. More often he was the one who might say, "I don't know," if he said anything. Or he would stare at the wall or turn the TV on and begin flipping the channels. Sometimes he would simply get up and leave the room as Kimberly raged at him. Occasionally he would try to defuse the situation by saying something like "uh-huh" as an attempt to calm Kimberly by agreeing with her. But anything he did was motivated by his attempt to avoid the situation and to keep himself from feeling any emotion on his part. He was in the freeze mode of fear.

What brought them to counseling was what Jerry did during their last argument. Not only did he walk out of the room, but he left the house and was gone for several hours. Basically, from all outward appearances, emotion lived only on one side of their marriage—Kimberly's.

Jerry's side of the marriage was like an emotional desert. He thought he had long ago locked his emotions into a safe place, somewhere he couldn't get hurt again. He had learned how to stay away from his emotions, and he wished Kimberly would do the same. He didn't realize he was trapped by the emotion of fear. And what seemed to make no sense to him was that the less emotion he invested in the marriage, the more emotional Kimberly became. He didn't realize that for her, their marriage felt so empty that she wondered just who Jerry was—she felt like she hardly knew him.

Every time Kimberly lost her temper, she would later ruminate for hours, berating herself, trying to understand what had set her off. She promised herself that she would stay in control of her emotions in the future. But even when she was determined not to blow up, she would lose her temper and explode at Jerry. It seemed every time that happened, she would say things she later regretted. And recently, she blew up at Jerry and said some really ugly things about him that hurt him deeply. It was the first time in a long time that Kimberly saw an emotional response from him. Jerry used that episode to blame her for all their problems.

In each of these examples, the individuals say that they truly love each other. But for love to grow, the skill of traveling in the land of the negative emotions must be acquired. Only then does love have meaning. The good news is, any one of these couples can learn the skills of SMART Love. And so can you.

How It All Goes Wrong

None of these couples married with any thought that they might have trouble in their relationship when it came to their emotions. In fact, early in the relationship, they were each able to make the other person feel important enough that there was a peaceful calm to the relationship. They could talk together without either one losing control of their emotions. In addition, Pat and Kimberly had felt connected to their husbands. They seldom felt the need to hide something from them or criticize them in the hope that things would get better. They both felt they were truly being helpful in the suggestions they frequently handed out to their husbands. Things were good back then. Neither Don nor Jerry realized that they were missing out on life because they were controlled by their fear. To them, that was just the way they were, and what they'd grown up with as they observed their parents. The same goes for Angie's seemingly emotionless parents.

Early in a couple's relationship, especially before the wedding and soon after, a man takes the time to calm his future wife and is basically able to soothe any anxiety she is experiencing. He easily engages her in conversation, and he truly believes and communicates to her that she is important to him. He knows how to express that to her. But as the marriage moves forward in time, he may gradually become more and more distracted by work and the success he begins to feel on the job. Or he may get caught up in the success or failure of his favorite sports team, or in the distraction of his hobby—be it hunting, fishing, golf, or something else. He once looked at his home as a place where he could relax, but her "helpful criticisms" make it less and less relaxing to be there. He begins to feel that no matter how much effort he makes in the marriage, it will never be enough.

For the woman, those early days of the relationship are great because her future husband makes her feel she is connected to him, and he talks with her at length. Her basic understanding of what she wants in a spouse is to be with someone with whom she can interact. Interacting makes her feel connected to him. Little does she know that her need for him to talk would feel like pressure to him, and it would begin to trigger his sense of shame at his failure to be what she wants him to be. Her "helpful criticisms" only add to his shame of being a failure. Neither of them realizes that a man's core fear is becoming a failure, and his natural response is to protect himself by closing down. As he withdraws, she begins to feel more and more disconnected from him, and that just feeds into her core fear, which is to be shut off from her husband—to be disconnected.

Even though a wife may have a network of female friends with whom she can talk, it just isn't the same. She wants him to talk to her and wants him to actively listen when she talks to him. She wants to feel a connection with him, and she feels talking is the path to that connection. But now the only time they talk is when he is angry or when she is fed up.

Add to all of this the differences in how a man and a woman view emotions. It all starts on the playground. What do most little boys love to do? Be active! Whatever game they play, they will ignore their emotions and enjoy playing. Most little girls don't need to be so active, so they enjoy sitting on the sidelines "relating." They talk about what they are feeling. That's why they have slumber parties—so they can relate to each other. Not one of our sons asked to have a slumber party, nor do I remember them ever being invited to one.

So when a couple gets married, the wife may know how to talk about feelings and emotions, and the husband may know how to be active in sports or work hard at his job. He needs to slowly ease his way into any area of emotions. But because she is more familiar with the world of emotions, she gets anxious with his discomfort, and her frustration leads her to what is called a "harsh start-up" of a conversation, as opposed to a "soft start-up." In a harsh start-up, the wife jumps into the issue at full speed emotionally. In addition, she knows the language of the emotions, whereas for the man, the language of emotions is often like learning a second language—he doesn't know the vocabulary.

That's why Don eventually shuts Pat out and leaves her alone with her hurt and anger. Jerry ends up doing the same thing—he just does it from the beginning of the would-be conversation. And Angie's parents have no clue as to how their lack of skill to navigate the land of emotions hurts Angie and isolates them from one another. For a positive end result to these situations, each person has to learn how to recognize and manage their emotions. Learning how to navigate their world of emotions by developing the skills of SMART Love will transform their relationships.

It's How We Are Wired

What Don and Pat didn't know was that their problem is universal and is based on how our brains work. They didn't know that whenever we see or hear something, that information, as we said earlier, is sent directly to the emotional part of our brain. The emotional brain is designed to protect us from any threat, even when the threat we perceive is coming from our spouse. It's our warning system that prepares our body to fight, take flight, or freeze. In other words, we are wired to experience anger and fear.

Pat was already on guard with Don, and just his walking into the room set off within her a warning signal to get ready for trouble. She would have fled the room if that had been possible, but instead she froze in place and prepared for the fight. Don came into the room, his emotional brain sensed the tension, and he quickly geared up for a fight. He had trained his emotional brain to be extra sensitive to any perceived threat.

Kimberly and Jerry had a different routine. Kimberly's brain operates much like Don's in that she is always on the lookout for potential problems, and her preferred response is to fight. Jerry's warning system is overly sensitized in the other direction. It's almost as if he had shut down his emotional brain and depended solely on his rational brain. Every perception of a potential threat triggers in him the response to take flight, and he usually does that by withdrawing into himself.

Both of Angie's parents had learned at an early age to be afraid of their emotional brains. To them, feeling anything only led to hurt and disappointment. While they enjoyed the emotions they felt during their dating and engagement, it didn't take them long to revert to their old pattern of perceiving everything they experienced through the rational part of their brains. There is no war going on in their brains— the emotional brain had conceded and surrendered to fear! There was no out-of-control expression of emotions, only the controlling power of their fear.

Pat, Don, and Kimberly each experienced an emotional hijacking in that the information they perceived was never processed and passed on to the rational part of the brain. That's why after most couples have a fight, they later feel it was irrational. And it was! "We argued about *that*?" they say to themselves, and maybe they even say it to their spouse. Or they ask themselves, "Why are we so fearful when it comes to interacting?" Then they end up berating themselves for either freezing or losing control and determine to stay calm and get involved in a healthy conversation the next time. But left to human nature, the next time will be much like the first.

What about Shame and Sadness?

We've looked at how anger and fear are wired into our brains, but let's look at the two basic emotions that we have to learn: shame and sadness. These also affect our relationships. There are two kinds of shame—rightful shame, which is a form of genuine guilt, and toxic shame, which leads to consistent feelings of false guilt. Rightful shame is what we feel when we've done something wrong or embarrassing. Toxic shame is shame unrelated to any current behaviors or misdeeds. Many of us struggle with feelings of toxic shame but don't understand why we feel it. Its roots go back to early experiences that we barely remember. There is nothing in the present that gives a rational basis for our feeling toxic shame. In spite of that, we interact with others out of a position of one-down, and we feel like we are the bad person in the interaction. We may have no awareness that the shame we struggle with is toxic. As a result, it colors our experiences, leading us to a fearful posture in relationship to others. We say things and do things that reflect that emotion, but we can't put a label on any of our current behaviors as being the cause of our feeling toxic shame.

Sadness is an important part of the grieving process, just as anger is a protest against loss. But sadness can also be a learned emotional stance when it is experienced as a persistent state. Over time, it shows itself as a general melancholy or a somber mood that persists. Or it can be diagnosed as a state of dysthymia, which is a persistent mild form of depression. Sadness can also be an ongoing condition of pessimism. People who experience sadness as their basic emotion probably grew up in a very negative, "glass is always empty, or at best only half full" experience in their family.

When our perceptions stay in the emotional brain and don't get sent to the rational brain for evaluation, it is usually because we're holding on to our experience of one or more of the negative emotions. So our experience of anger, fear, sadness, and/or shame doesn't get processed. These negative emotions disrupt our marriage relationship and undo any hard work we have invested in building a strong marriage. And it happens so quickly that it surprises us. We need more than a vow to ourselves that "we'll never do that again." We have to learn now to stop and recognize this as a vicious cycle. Once we allow our negative emotions to rule, it becomes easier to fall into the same old pattern again and again. That's why we need to learn how our emotions work the way they do—we have to become emotionally intelligent in order to experience SMART Love!

The Land of Emotions

Let's describe this incredible land of emotions. Emotions form the foundation of who we are, for our emotions are closest to our innermost being. They bring Technicolor to our lives. Researchers generally agree that we experience six primary emotions: anger, sadness, joy, surprise, shame (sometimes called disgust), and fear. Surprisingly, love doesn't appear on the list. We'll see later why love is our goal and how it is more than just an emotion.

As we explore these six basic emotions, the first step will be learning what to call them. Each emotion has a "family" of feelings and moods. For example, take the emotion of anger. We can experience the emotion of anger in a wide range. We can feel furious, outraged, seething, upset, mad, frustrated, annoyed, or irritated, plus other nuances of these emotions. These are the *feelings* associated with anger. The *mood* associated with an emotion is simply a generalized pervasive feeling. So the mood associated with the emotion of anger is simply a generalized feeling of being upset, uptight, or touchy that is pervasive over time.

Fear can also be experienced in various ways as feelings and moods, and at different levels of intensity. We can feel terrified, panicky, frantic, threatened, insecure, cautious, unsure, or simply worried. The moods associated with fear are a generalized anxiety, being cautious, or a pervasive experience of feeling uneasy or nervous.

Or take the emotion of sadness. It can be as strong as feeling depressed, alone, dejected, miserable, or hopeless. But it can also be experienced as feeling distressed, somber, unhappy, upset, or disappointed. Moods that would fit the emotion of sadness are general melancholy or a very somber view of life overall.

Shame also has its shadings of expression. It can be as strong as feeling worthless, disgraced, defamed, or dishonored. But it can also be experienced as feeling unworthy, guilty, embarrassed, or uncomfortable. The general moods associated with shame could be expressed as a lack of confidence, a general sense of feeling worthless, or even extreme hesitance and bashfulness.

So an emotion is the overarching experience of joy, surprise, anger, fear, sadness, or shame. A feeling is how we experience the nuance of the emotion in the here and now. It is also the word used to describe a mood, which is a feeling we hold on to over a period of time.

Below is a chart that shows the four basic negative emotions and some of the possible feeling and mood words associated with each, with the more intense ones at the top.

The negative emotions are the only ones we will look at, as they are the ones we need help with. As you practice naming what you are feeling, you will begin to understand the nuances of each feeling or mood you are experiencing. Make a copy of the word list and learn to identify and name what you feel.

Anger	Fear	Sadness	Shame
Furious	Terrified	Depressed	Sorrowful
Enraged	Scared	Alone	Worthless
Irate	Petrified	Hurt	Disgraced
Seething	Panicky	Hopeless	Mortified
Upset	Apprehensive	Somber	Apologetic
Frustrated	Frightened	Distressed	Unworthy
Annoyed	Nervous	Moody	Embarrassed
Irritated	Timid	Blue	Regretful
Touchy	Anxious	Disappointed	Uncomfortable

An interesting fact about the land of emotions is that there is a unique facial expression for each of the negative emotions. Author Paul Ekman has led the way in this research.[1] The positive emotions as they appear on the face are not threatening, so they are easier to identify—most of us can recognize the facial expressions associated with joy and surprise. But growing more intelligent in the land of emotions means that we identify how we handle the negative feelings, moods, and emotions. One way to become more emotionally intelligent is to learn to recognize the negative emotions of anger, fear, sadness, and shame as they show on the face.

I often tell men to study the expressions on their wives' faces. When they see a look they can't identify, I tell them to stop and ask her what she was just feeling. Then make a note of it in their "research journal" so when they see that look again, they can identify it. Husbands are usually perplexed at the good response they get from their wives when they tell them they are trying to read their emotions.

Since each of the basic emotions represents a family of feelings, they can also be expressed in up or down moods. So experiencing SMART Love means we first identify the negative emotions in ourselves and then identify the most common feelings we experience that come from those emotions. When we are able to name our emotions and feelings, we will also be able to name our moods. For example, we can learn to recognize the difference between being annoyed and being furious when we experience those feelings. We begin to see quickly that they are both associated with the emotion of anger.

We all have subconscious ways we manage most of our moods. If we are tired and feeling down, we know if we call a friend and meet for coffee or ice cream, our mood will probably be lifted. If our friend doesn't respond positively or is unavailable, it can deepen our down mood. Moods can be influenced easily by our actions and words. But emotions and the feelings associated with them are more entrenched and don't easily change with our activities. These three things—emotions with the consequence of feelings and moods—make up the landscape of the world of emotions.

The Problem for Men

Men can be at a disadvantage when it comes to SMART Love. As boys, they were most likely taught by their parents and/or their peers to hide their emotions. The only exception is the emotion of anger. Anger is okay for men to experience, but only in the right places. For example, if an eleven-year-old boy is playing in his Little League baseball game, and he is so ashamed when he strikes out that he cries, his dad and perhaps even his mother may be mortified. They may sit in embarrassed silence. Or maybe Dad will quietly confront his son and tell him to act like a man. The other boys on the team don't know how to handle it either, so most of them will just ignore it or tease the "crybaby."

But if he strikes out, gets mad, and throws his bat against the fence or slings his helmet to the ground, his parents may sigh and say to each other, "Ah, that's my boy!" Anger is an okay emotion for men and boys, but they're not taught how they can manage and express it.

In my counseling room, I often ask a husband, "What are you feeling right now?" as his wife sits next to him in tears. He can't say that he's angry, because he's probably the cause of his wife's tears. He sits in silence for a moment, then typically answers, "Well, I think—" and I interrupt. I emphasize, "I don't want to know what you think; I want to know what you *feel* right now." And there is a long silence. Men know how to think but often are at a loss when asked to describe what they feel. I use this as an opportunity to show that the husband has feelings; he just doesn't have the language to identify or describe them. So we go through a list of feeling words, and he is able to say yes to those connected to what he is feeling and no to those not connected. I do this exercise in part because I want his wife to learn to recognize his inability to self-generate the language of emotions.

Men are at another disadvantage in that their brains are designed to listen in order to fix whatever is wrong. Their brains are not designed to have a conversation about feelings for conversation's sake. It drives a wife crazy because all she wants her husband to do is listen to her and seek to understand the heart of what she is saying. She doesn't want him to try to fix the situation, even though that is his natural bent.

The Problem for Women

Anger is not very ladylike. It's okay for little girls to cry, but to be angry—no way. I've talked with women who should be angry, but all they can do is feel sadness. For a quick moment, some might experience anger as a protest, but it doesn't last very long before the tears take over again.

The other problem women face when learning the principles of SMART Love is that they don't know how to relate to the different way their husbands talk and listen. For her, talking is the way to stay connected to him. For him, talking is a means to fixing a problem. As a result, she often doesn't know how to respond when he either wants to fix the problem or doesn't want to talk. So gradually she becomes more critical—something she would never do or ever need to do when facing misunderstandings with her female friends. In her mind, her criticism is designed to strengthen or repair the marriage. But the more critical she becomes, the more she pushes him away and ends up feeling disconnected. SMART Love is designed for both the husband and the wife to understand their own natural tendencies whenever they are in the land of emotions.

SMART Love

SMART Love is based on four big ideas regarding how both a wife and a husband can learn to experience connection and peace in their marriage.

1. With SMART Love, you will each learn how to *regulate your emotional self*. When you are able to identify your emotions and feelings, you will become more grown-up in your relationship with each other. The skills you develop will make you instantly aware of what you are feeling as you begin to feel it. You will develop a new ability to name your emotions and manage them before they have done harm to the relationship.

Part of self-awareness involves being able to understand how our buttons get pushed. So much of how we react to each other is a continuation of patterns that were set in place when we were young. When we're adults, these reactions often become automatic. Recognizing the expression of our emotions also includes the idea of understanding and dealing with the roots of our typical tendencies.

2. With SMART Love, you will each learn how to *break the cycles* that are so entrenched in your marriage relationship. Most arguments are basically an attempt to define who is right and who is wrong. That's always a losing pattern of behavior. Even if you are right, you don't win. It's a fact that most couples coming to marital counseling have an agenda. Both the husband and the wife come with the intent of proving to the counselor that "I am right and my spouse is wrong!"

It's so easy to get caught up in the blame game, even when we know that resolving who is to blame accomplishes nothing except to add hurt to each spouse. After all, we will still be left with the task of resolving the problem behaviors. Most marital counselors are able to see through the effort to place blame and get to the cycles of behavior that need to be broken. With SMART Love, you will develop strategies and behaviors that will help you know how to change your negative cycles and manage your emotions, even when you are caught in a seemingly no-win situation.

3. SMART Love will help you *restore the connection* you had with each other. Being connected to your spouse was a legitimate expectation when you got married. You felt it before the wedding. But for many, that expectation gradually slips away as time passes.

Connection in your marriage is built in the land of emotions. It is based first on being emotionally available to each other. The more uncomfortable we are with each other's emotions, as well as with our own, the less we are emotionally available. We have to break free from old patterns so we can be open to each other.

The second part of a connection is being emotionally responsive to each other. In the previous chapter, we met Jerry. He was too afraid to respond to Kimberly, and that was a major factor in their disconnection from each other. When we expand our ability to manage what we experience emotionally, we become more responsive to each other.

The third part of what constitutes a connection is acceptance, being increasingly able not only to accept the emotions of your spouse but to identify with them. All three are necessary components of an emotional connection.

4. SMART Love ultimately allows you to *embrace love*. Everyone says they got married because they were in love. As we pointed out earlier, none of the lists of emotions include love. It is typically seen in research as not being a primary emotion but rather a secondary emotion that is based on our emotional responses to loving behaviors. As we will see in the next chapter, love is the most important emotion, for it is the one God intended us to experience. When we become

emotionally SMART, loving behaviors increase, and that allows a couple to more fully embrace the feelings of love.

SMART Love is about gaining the ability to identify your own emotions, but equally important, it's about learning how to identify your spouse's emotions. It includes the ability to empathize with what your spouse is feeling, just as you identify your own emotions as they are happening. It also means you can use the information gained from observing your spouse's emotions to regulate your own, and ultimately to manage successfully the emotional climate in your marriage and your family.

SMART Love is different from IQ. SMART Love is an intangible, which makes it difficult to measure. So there is no generally recognized SMART Love test that places your score in relation to other people's. (An official Emotional Intelligence Appraisal is available from www.talentsmart.com, which is primarily oriented to the business world.)

Also, IQ refers to your ability to learn things, which does not change based on what you have learned. It stays pretty much the same throughout your life. In contrast, the ability to love SMART is changeable. You will increase your EQ as you learn to put into practice the skills of SMART Love. So if you are not very SMART in your marriage, you can become very SMART!

The Skills of SMART Love

Two of the competencies we will develop in SMART Love are personal—they develop within us individually. Three of them are relational. All of them are interactive. Competence in the personal skills is foundational and involves becoming knowledgeable about the common language of emotions.

First, you will be able to describe an emotion as you become more aware of what you are experiencing emotionally in the situation. As a result, you will become more skillful at being able to appropriately manage your own emotions in a conflict situation.

Think back on the three case studies in the first chapter. No one in these examples was able to describe what they were feeling in the situation, and none of them, even Angie's mom and dad, were able to appropriately manage their emotions. Pat and Don were both out of control with their anger, as was Kimberly. Jerry and Angie's parents were completely unable to express any emotion since they were so bound up by their fear. The foundational step for each person begins with becoming aware of what they are experiencing emotionally and being able to identify what basic negative emotion they seem to fall into.

Then comes the second personal skill, which is being able to manage strong emotions as they are identified and occur. If we can't identify our emotions, we will not be able to manage them. Most of us simply give in to the emotion and then wish we had just ignored what we felt. Or we ignore the emotion because of our fear of the consequences of dealing with it.

As personal foundational skills become stronger, competency in the relational area develops. The third skill is relational and focuses on being accountable to each other as a couple and to someone else for how you are handling your emotions.

35

Fourth, you will be able to empathize more with your spouse, which includes not only having the ability to read what they are feeling but also experiencing those feelings as if you were in their shoes.

Finally, the fifth skill is for both of you to become comfortable and relaxed as you travel together in the land of emotions. No longer will it be a scary and strange land.

Before we look in depth at the basic skills of SMART Love, let's do an appraisal of where each of you is in relation to the five skills of SMART Love.

The SMART Love Inventory

As we mentioned in chapter 1, SMART Love is based on five competencies: (1) becoming self-aware of your emotions; (2) managing your emotions; (3) accountability to yourself, your spouse, and others; (4) reading the other person's emotions; and (5) learning to live together in the land of emotions.

The first two competencies are skills we develop within ourselves; they are personal skills. The third relates to how comfortable we are emotionally with friends. The other two skills are interactive and interpersonal skills that we develop by building on the first three.

Below is an inventory to help you know how skillful you are at this point in experiencing and expressing SMART Love. Make a photocopy so you and your spouse can each take the inventory. (Note: You can also take the inventory free of charge at www.smartlove.us.)

This inventory will ask you to respond to a statement that describes your typical behavior. Take your time to get a clear picture of what the statement is saying, then answer as honestly as you can, thinking in terms of how you are most of the time. There are no *never* or *always* answers, so that makes it easier to think in terms of *mostly*.

As you respond to each statement, think of it in general terms. Don't think of it as describing something that happened in a specific situation two days ago.

The scoring is based on three responses. Make your choice by entering the number 3 for "usually," 2 for "sometimes," and 1 for "seldom." In the first column, answer in terms of how you see yourself. In the second column, answer in terms of how you see your spouse.

SMART Love Inventory

Usually—3 points Sometimes—2 points Seldom—1 point	How I See Myself	How I See My Spouse
1. I am aware of my emotions.	2	3
2. I can express my feelings appropriately.	2	3
3. I am able to observe myself when I am emotional.	2	3
4. I can soothe myself when anxious.	3	2
5. I am accepting of my moods, both good and bad.	3	2
6. I do not worry.	2	2
7. I am attuned to my values.	3	3
8. I am able to keep quiet when I know talking won't help.	2	1

	Usually—3 points Sometimes—2 points Seldom—1 point	How I See Myself	How I See My Spouse
9.	I know what pushes my buttons.	3	3
10.	I am comfortable with change.	1	3
11.	I can acknowledge my shortcomings.	2	3
12.	I am generally an optimist.	3	3
13.	I have a sense of humor about myself.	3	3
14.	Down moods don't last very long for me.	2	3
15.	I am generally a confident person.	2	3
16.	I am able to control my anger.	2	3
17.	I do not get overwhelmed by my emotions.	3	3
18.	I do not say things when I'm upset that I later regret.	2	3
19.	I am aware of a wide range of feelings.	3	3
20.	I am not controlled by my emotions.	2	3
21.	I have at least one friend who knows when I'm hurting.	1	2
22.	I can talk to others about what I am feeling.	2	2
23.	I can empathize with my friends' emotional issues.	3	1
24.	It is easy for me to share my fears with my friends.	2	3
25.	I believe "family secrets" can be shared with trusted friends.	2	1
26.	I have friends who share with me their emotional ups and downs.	3	3
27.	I am open to my spouse's comments about me.	2	3
28.	My spouse and I are comfortable talking directly with each other.	3	3
29.	I can feel what my spouse feels.	2	3

	How I See Myself	How I See My Spouse
Usually—3 points *Sometimes—2 points* *Seldom—1 point*	3	3
30. My spouse and I know how to show each other we care.		
31. I can hear what's behind the words my spouse says.	3	3
32. My spouse and I share a vision for our marriage.	3	3
33. I can stay calm in the midst of turmoil.	2	3
34. My spouse and I are both good negotiators.	3	2
35. I am a great listener with my spouse.	3	3
36. I can balance my needs with my spouse's needs.	2	3
37. Even when I don't agree, my spouse knows I understand.	3	3
38. As a couple, we are a team.	3	3
39. We have close friends as a couple.	3	3
40. I understand how my childhood experiences have affected me as an adult.	3	2

Self-Awareness score is based on the odd-numbered statements 1–19.

My Score: 21

My Spouse's Score: 24

Managing Your Emotions score is based on the even-numbered statements 2–20.

My Score: 23

My Spouse's Score: 24

Accountability score is based on statements 21–26.

My Score: 13

My Spouse's Score: 17

Reading the Other Person's Emotions score is based on the odd-numbered statements 27–39.

My Score: 18

My Spouse's Score: 23

Together in the Land of Emotions score is based on the even-numbered statements 28–40.

My Score: 20

My Spouse's Score: 19

My Total Score: 161

My Spouse's Total Score: 169

The lowest possible total score is 40 points, and the highest possible score is 120 points. If you scored a total of 60 or less, you have your work cut out for you. You may even work hard at avoiding feeling emotions. If you scored between 60 and 90, you're somewhat comfortable with some emotions but avoid others. If you scored over 90, then you probably are comfortable with your emotional words and pretty much know the emotional landscape.

Now that you've scored your inventory, share all of your scores with your spouse. Remember, you are embarking *together* on the journey to develop SMART Love, so you're going to need to work through this process together.

However, be careful as you share how you scored each other. When you hear your spouse's score and compare it to how you scored him or her, you may think, *That can't be!* Your spouse is probably thinking the same thing about your scores. So don't even go there! It's important to remember that everyone has a tendency to overestimate their own abilities when it comes to their emotions and to underestimate their spouse's.

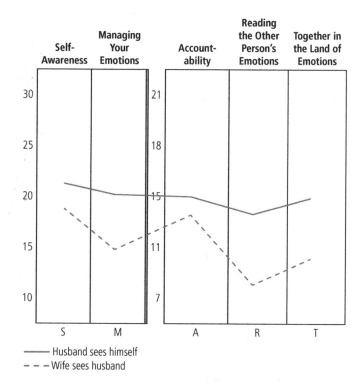

—— Husband sees himself
- - - Wife sees husband

Following the example above, plot your scores on the graph on the next page, using one color to show how you scored yourself and a different color to show how your spouse scored you. Have your spouse do the same. For example, if you scored 19 on "Self-Awareness," place a dot at the approximate value of 19. If you scored 15 on "Managing Your Emotions," place a dot at the approximate value of 15. Do the same with "Accountability," "Reading the Other Person's Emotions," and "Together in the Land of Emotions."

Connect the five dots for each as you see in the example. This will show you where you are weak and where you are strong, and where you think your spouse is weak and strong.

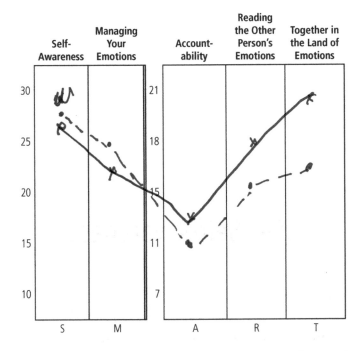

This will give you a picture of how skilled you are with SMART Love. It will also give you a reality check in how your spouse sees you.

This just gives you a map of how comfortable you are in the land of emotions. After working through some of the Action Plans, you may want to retake the inventory. But the real work lies ahead.

S—Self-Awareness

Self-awareness is the foundation and starting point of SMART Love. The skills of SMART Love are built on how aware we are of ourselves. Self-awareness goes beyond just being aware of our emotions to being aware of the many complexities that make up who we are as God's incredible creation. It involves being able to clearly articulate our values; know what's really important in our lives; understand our tendencies in certain situations; and identify our dreams, goals, and desires for our future. It's the ability to more fully know ourselves from the inside out.

Self-awareness takes time. But our way of life typically does not allow much time or space for introspection. Our lives are too busy, and we end up overwhelmed by all the things that need to be done on a day-to-day basis. We only have time to react to the pressures of the moment, and there are plenty of those lined up ready to grab our attention. We get up early, grab breakfast after attempting to exercise, help get breakfast for the kids, and quickly check our emails before heading to the office or taking the kids to school. It hardly seems like the day has started and then the kids are home. We plan a meal or quickly grab takeout, straighten up the house, pay the bills, mow the lawn, help the kids with homework, and finish some project we started on the weekend. Then, if we have time, we can crash and watch some TV.

The weekends aren't much different. There are projects that need to be attended to, and we shop for food, wash and gas up the cars, and maybe, if we can, hit a movie. Add to the list all the other things we "ought" to be doing—things our parents taught us to do, our boss needs us to do, or our pastor is "expecting" us to do—and is it any wonder that most of us live what is called "the unexamined life"? The feeling that we are nothing but human *doers* is really quite an accurate description of how we end up. What ever happened to our living as a human *being*? We just don't have enough time to worry about that!

Gradually over time, we lose the sense of who we really are and even the sense of what is really important to us. It's not that all our busyness is invested in unimportant things. It's more that we don't have the time to look inward and remember that our dreams, our values, and our feelings were about what we used to think was really important. When we are forced to slow down and reflect on our lives, we don't really like what we see. We feel trapped, we get antsy, and worst of all, we don't know how to break out of the cycle of busyness.

The cost we pay for our busyness—when we live like we are "human doers"—is that we will eventually prioritize our work, our kids, our friends, our church, and even our extended family over our marriage. In spite of what we tell ourselves, we will push our marriage off to the side and tell ourselves we'll deal with it when we have more time. We know marriage takes work, but we don't have time for that much effort right now. Maybe later, when the kids are grown and the finances are more stable, we'll have the time and the energy to work on our relationship. But in the here and now, since we don't have time, we end up simply reacting as we struggle with understanding the emotions of our spouse, our kids, our co-workers, and even ourselves.

As human doers, we also live in a state of emotional and spiritual deficit. It's hard to "be with" someone; it's much easier to "do for" someone. We "do" for our kids, our boss, our co-workers, our spouse, even God. We fool ourselves about the relationships we think we have through social media, as we spend time texting, on Facebook, or on whatever the latest social media trend happens to be. If we are alone for a moment without our smartphones, we realize we have a pervasive lack of self-awareness—we can't define what's really important to us beyond the moment. This is especially true when it comes to our inability to experience any positive emotions. What we do experience are the negative emotions of fear, sadness, shame, and anger. Eventually, we will end up becoming controlled by either our fear or our anger, and/or we fall into depression as we struggle with a sense of guilt and shame over not doing enough.

We find ourselves having a short fuse, always hurrying, our mind always racing, especially when we are trying to go to sleep. We're easily triggered by other people, especially our spouse, and we say things we later regret. No matter how hard we try, we can't seem to catch up. We feel a lot like Paul when he said, "I don't really understand myself, for I want to do what is right, but I don't do it. Instead, I do what I hate. . . . I don't want to do what is wrong, but I do it anyway" (Rom. 7:15, 19). So what do we do? There is an answer.

Self-Awareness—the Path to Emotional Health

All of what we've described so far is what happens to us when we are lacking in self-awareness. Self-awareness is basically a sense of knowing yourself. God's desire for us is that we know ourselves. Paul says not to "think you are better than you really are. Be honest in your evaluation of yourselves" (Rom. 12:3). I have to know myself in order to honestly evaluate myself.

Add to this Socrates's admonition to "know thyself," and we have the starting point for change. To know ourselves is another way of saying we are to become more and more self-aware. It's the skill we can and must develop, as it affects every relationship we have as human beings. It involves a myriad of things—we must know our values, our dreams and desires, and our emotions. That's the goal if we are to be all that God meant us to be.

But first, in order to begin the process of knowing ourselves better, we must make the effort to slow down our lives. How do we do that when there are so many demands on our time? If slowing down sounds impossible to you, start by answering the following question: What pressures or demands make it so hard for you to slow down?

Take some time, think it through, and write down your answers, then evaluate and prioritize them. Ask yourself what

47

stops you from dropping the demands on your time that are at the bottom of your list. In fact, let's be bold: move the bottom three things on your list to a "do not do" list!

Second, evaluate your ability to experience what is called your "observing ego." How aware are you of the part that is able to watch yourself? Author William Styron described his battle with a deep and pervasive depression, the sense that he was always "being accompanied by a second self."[1] That was the way he described his observing ego. It was a part of himself that he could watch and talk to about what he was doing or thinking.

Most of us are aware, to some degree, of having a "second self" whose main purpose is to observe ourselves. It is a part of us that is developed as we are growing up, and it is basically our ability to step back from an experience and be able to evaluate ourselves as if we were watching from outside ourselves. We see what we just said or just did, or how we reacted to what just happened. It includes the idea that we are able to have a conversation with ourselves about our emotions, our tendencies, and our behaviors.

The third part of this process is to be able to articulate your core values. What is most important to you? What matters the most to you? This is not as easy as it sounds. One man said that his wife was the most important thing in his life. She protested by saying that his work was more important to him. To her, he worked hard because it was his priority— the most important thing in his life. She challenged him by reminding him that if she died, he would still be working. As we talked about it together, he was able to see his wife's point, but then added, "You are the one who gives meaning to my working hard." His struggle was to become more aware of the reality of how he balanced his priorities between his wife and his work, and to become more aware of how his behavior affected her.

Another man said to his wife, "You are my priority." When I asked her where she thought she was on his priority list, she said, "I may be as high as number five, but no higher." I pressed him by asking, "Why do you think your wife puts herself at number five on your priority list and you say she's number one?" He couldn't come up with any answer. He wasn't aware of what he was doing that led her to feel that way. He had to first deal with the reality that she felt she was fifth, regardless of where he thought he placed her. That was her experience of him, her reality of their relationship. As they engaged in some honest discussion together, they both became more aware of not only themselves but also how they affected each other in their marriage.

Self-Awareness Defined

We've been talking about self-awareness in general, as it is part of our emotional growth process. Now let's look at self-awareness in reference to SMART Love. In that context, it means we begin to develop a greater awareness of our own emotions as we experience them in the moment. It includes the idea of understanding our behavioral tendencies when we experience a particular feeling or emotion and being able to stay on top of our reactions.

Obviously, the issue of self-awareness goes beyond what we are feeling emotionally. Let's consider how emotions affected Don, Pat, and Kimberly from chapter 1. They seemed to have access to their world of emotions, but they lost control as they got caught up in the emotional outbursts of their anger. Later, they might have felt some shame as they regretted what they said or did. They couldn't recognize an emotion when it was happening, nor could they manage what they were experiencing emotionally before it took over. Obviously, they were not very aware of who they were and didn't know what was really important to them.

Angie's parents and Jerry might have thought they were more in control of themselves since they had long ago shut off their emotions. They might have actually believed they could survive in an emotionless place. The truth is, they did not possess self-awareness in general, and when it came to feelings and emotions, they were clueless. If they were honest, they would tell you that the only emotion they actually didn't allow themselves to experience was anger. In the end, they were controlled by their fear and their shame, and they struggled with depression.

It seemed obvious that Don, Pat, and Kimberly could sense they were becoming angry and knew they were angry when the conflict started. But they were unaware of their behavioral tendencies related to how they would react to their anger. Only in reflecting later could they see how their anger controlled them and their behavior. When they were first becoming angry, they simply reacted. It's almost like their anger suddenly appeared out of thin air and took control. And even though Pat was trying to stay calm, her anger quickly controlled her as she reacted to Don's anger.

There is a principle that says we cannot tame our emotions unless we can name them. We've already noted that men often struggle more than women with being able to name what they are feeling. They generally hide their emotions, and they also deny them. To the typical man, becoming emotional is a sign of weakness or of a loss of self-control. So the first task for men is to learn how to name their emotions. To help in that, let's look again at the chart from chapter 2 that describes some of the feelings associated with the four core negative emotions. The feelings are arranged in intensity from top to bottom.

Anger	Fear	Sadness	Shame
Furious	Terrified	Depressed	Sorrowful
Enraged	Scared	Alone	Worthless
Irate	Petrified	Hurt	Disgraced
Seething	Panicky	Hopeless	Mortified
Upset	Apprehensive	Somber	Apologetic
Frustrated	Frightened	Distressed	Unworthy
Annoyed	Nervous	Moody	Embarrassed
Irritated	Timid	Blue	Regretful
Touchy	Anxious	Disappointed	Uncomfortable

Once you and your spouse are able to name the feeling or emotion, the second step is to begin to think about what you are experiencing when you feel it. This is part of the reason why you will need to slow down. It's not a typical behavior to think about what you're feeling or to ask what you're thinking about what you're feeling. However, try to identify what kind of thoughts trigger that emotion or feeling. This is especially important when a feeling seems to come out of nowhere—suddenly it is there and it is intense. But it didn't just appear; there was a trigger.

Our emotions are triggered by the part of the brain called the limbic system and, in particular, a small part of that system called the amygdala. The amygdala is our warning system, and it is connected to our left prefrontal cortex—the decision part of our brain. The amygdala is designed to prepare us to meet some threat through either the emotion of anger or the emotion of fear. That's why one of those negative emotions will typically be our basic go-to stance emotionally when we are stressed. Early in our lives, emotional patterns are established as we approach perceived threats with either an angry response or a fearful response. Over time, pathways develop in our brain that instantly lead us to experience anger or fear when we feel threatened in any way. The threat could be as simple as being misunderstood.

Our Basic Emotional Posture

We typically choose to go to one of the basic four emotions when we are under stress, or when someone has pushed our buttons. We call that our "basic emotional posture," or BEP. There is usually a history to what primary negative feeling we experience, especially when it can make us feel so out of control. Identifying and understanding what our fallback emotion is will involve some historical remembering. For example, if you have a tendency to become angry as opposed to fearful, where and how did that begin? How did that pattern develop? What's at the root of your anger?

If your basic approach to the stressors of life is to experience fear, how did that come to be? Can you remember feeling fearful as a child? Which parent showed their fear more? How did that same pattern develop in you? If your basic emotional posture takes you instantly to toxic shame, you must have grown up being shamed. Who was the primary person putting you down? Who always made you feel like you were less than the others in your family? Or was it a general pattern where everyone shamed everyone else?

Sadness, or depression, as a basic emotional posture is usually related to growing up in what is called a depressogenic environment. This is a term used primarily in relation to substances that make us feel depressed, such as alcohol. When you drink too much alcohol, you experience depression. A family can also be a depressogenic factor when one or both parents are depressed, and depression just seems to be the family's lot in life.

When we refer to our BEP, we are also, as mentioned earlier, talking about what are often called our buttons. Our buttons are our automatic responses to situations or people. They were programmed into our subconscious mind in the first six or seven years of life. Because our subconscious mind is so quick, it responds instantly to hurtful patterns of behavior that we are probably not even aware of until it happens. Our quick response reflects what we saw and experienced in relation to our parents and others during those early, formative years.

For example, if your basic approach to stress issues is to respond with fear, it is likely that your parents exhibited a lot of fearful responses to the issues of life, and they may have treated you in a way that made you fearful. Or if one or both of your parents were angry a lot, that's what got programmed into your subconscious mind. Understanding the roots of our automatic responses is an important part of becoming more self-aware emotionally. As we said, in order to become more self-aware, we have to take the time to think about our basic emotional posture, and we have to understand the roots of our emotions, as they set the stage for our behavioral tendencies.

Which is your basic emotional posture? Is it anger? Is it fear? Is it toxic shame? Or is it sadness and depression? Remember, our basic emotional posture is where we end up emotionally most of the time when under stress.

The Process

First, we are learning how to name an emotion, and second, we are taking the time to think about how we respond when we are experiencing that emotion. In other words, we are asking ourselves, "What am I feeling when I have that response, and what am I saying to myself?" Pat was able to do this once she could name the feeling of fear when Don questioned her. Then she had to identify what she was telling herself when she experienced fear, not only in relation to Don but in other situations as well.

The third part of our becoming emotionally healthier and more self-aware is to understand that our emotions have a purpose. There is always a reason for what we feel. That means we need to take the time to ask why, in the here and now, we are experiencing a particular emotion. If anger is our typical response to stressful situations, what is the purpose of it? In many cases, anger is used to push people or situations away. It's like we are saying, "I don't want to deal with this now, so I'll get angry and hopefully you will go away." Remember, though, there is a healthy side to the emotion of anger when it is experienced as a protest against some wrong.

Fear, on the other hand, doesn't push other people away. Its motivation is to prompt *us* to either freeze or run away.

Anger is movement against someone or something that is being perceived as a threat, while fear is our attempt to move away from someone or something that appears to be a threat. There is also a healthy side to fear that says, "The danger is too great; get away from here."

Fear and anger are the same in terms of what happens inside us physically. Let's say you are visiting an old friend who works in an inner-city ministry. He lives in a very unsafe neighborhood. He's busy in the evening, so he suggests you go sightseeing without him. "Just be back before 10:00 p.m. and you'll be safe," he tells you. Well, you get carried away and it's after 11:00 p.m. when you get to his place. You have to park several blocks away, so you say good-bye to the rental car—it'll probably be gone by morning.

As you walk toward your friend's apartment, you hear someone behind you. So you walk faster, and they walk faster too. Fear is a healthy emotion to experience as you begin to run and so does the other person. Just as you finally get to your friend's apartment and get the key in the door, the footsteps stop behind you, and your friend says, "Gotcha!"

You now joke that instantly he became your former friend, for the fear you had experienced moments earlier instantly shifted into anger. You were angry that you were set up by your friend. It wasn't funny to you. The point is, though, that your brain prepared you first to take flight and then, in a microsecond, shifted your fear into anger, preparing you to fight. But you didn't, and years later you laugh together about the experience.

When it comes to shame, there are two types we can experience. If we've done something we shouldn't have, we should experience genuine shame over our actions. For example, if we just told someone a bold-faced lie and we feel shame over it, that's genuine shame. Its purpose is to motivate us to make things right. This is a healthy experience of shame—there is something in the here and now that we are genuinely ashamed of, and rightfully so, and we need to repair what we've done.

The other type of shame is toxic shame, and when we experience it and examine why, we find there is really no valid reason for us to currently feel it. It's the type of shame we have in the present that is based on things we experienced in the past, such as things we were told while growing up. For example, we may still struggle with toxic shame because as kids we were told that we were worthless or wouldn't amount to anything. Those kinds of messages lead to a posture of toxic shame. If that posture is where we go in stressful situations, we need to identify its source and then argue against its validity. It is something we were taught, and it didn't come naturally!

If sadness is your basic emotional posture in life, its purpose is to get you to deal with the ungrieved losses you have experienced. Depression is usually tied to losses you have experienced in your primary relationships that you haven't grieved properly. To understand the roots of sadness and depression, you may need to talk with a professional counselor. The roots of depression are difficult to get access to, and understanding how they affect you is often too challenging to do alone.

The Importance of Moods

When we talk about our preferred stance in the face of stress, we can sometimes call that stance a mood. For example, if we typically go to anger as our predictable stance, we may be in a continual "irritable" or "touchy" mood. Or if we take fear as our basic stance, we may describe ourselves as having an anxious mood or having a feeling of our nerves constantly being on edge.

The feeling words can also describe our moods. It's important to note that our moods affect those around us. If I'm in an irritable mood, I will have an impact on my spouse and my family, and even my co-workers. Being self-aware emotionally means I am also aware of my moods as I experience them, and I take action to get out of that negative mood.

Several studies have demonstrated the power of a mood being transferred to others. In one study, three people were asked to sit together in silence in a small circle for one to two minutes. They found that the mood of the most emotionally expressive person was transmitted to the other two people even without a word being spoken. Another study noted that when a couple sits together silently for fifteen minutes, their heart rates and breathing rates become in sync with each other.

A Healthier Don and Pat

Let's assume that Don and Pat have been working on becoming more self-aware of their emotions. How might their conversation have gone if that were so?

Here are some of Pat's new thoughts: *Oh no, Don's home and I didn't get this finished. I'm feeling nervous because I don't want to set off an explosion.* (She can identify in the situation what she is experiencing emotionally.)

Don walks into the room and sees what Pat is doing, and he still asks, "What's that?"

Pat's response is clear and direct: "It's a gift for my mother, and I'm already feeling anxious thinking you're going to get upset about it." (She states and owns what she is feeling.)

Don's immediate reaction is to get defensive, but he is aware of that tendency, and he quickly puts a stop to those thoughts. Then he becomes aware of a growing feeling of anger as Pat's buying gifts for her mother touches on an old pattern that triggered their arguing in the past. He is still concerned about the fairness of how Pat treats the two mothers, but this time he says something like, "Wow, I don't want to go down the path of that old argument again. I started to get angry almost automatically, and I don't want to be angry. I hope you'll help me pick out something nice for my mother's birthday." (He also states and owns what he is feeling and is therefore able to avoid being controlled by his negative emotions.)

For both Don and Pat, being aware in the moment of what they were feeling helped them to stay calm. They were able to describe the feeling to the other person. They also realized they had choices in how to respond and were able to break free from some very destructive patterns. Pat owned her tension, and Don owned his experiencing the early stage of getting angry. They were able to show their care for each other as they built on the foundational principle of SMART Love—self-awareness.

So the question now is, how can we develop a greater sense of self-awareness in general and, more specifically, a greater awareness of our emotions? That is the purpose of the next chapter.

5

Self-Awareness Action Plans

Our goal now is to deepen our knowledge of ourselves, especially as it relates to our emotional self. We've noted how, in the busyness of our lives, we can easily lose touch with our real self. We all do to some degree. And as a result, we create an ideal self. For example, when someone asks, "How are you doing?" our ideal self answers without thinking, "Just fine, thank you. And how are you doing?" It's interesting to imagine what would happen if we suddenly started answering that question honestly. Perhaps people would stop asking it and come up with another question that doesn't expose the hiddenness of our real self.

Living with our ideal self reduces the need and eventually even the ability to practice self-reflection. We actually begin to believe we are doing "just fine, thank you." Our spouse can typically see through the facade of our ideal self, but they only challenge our reality when they are angry with us. At other times, they protect and accept our ideal self, hoping we will in turn accept their ideal self. But over time, living through our ideal selves leads us to a general dissatisfaction. Our marriage and our other relationships eventually seem unreal and superficial.

If, instead of living solely through our ideal self, our goal is to increase our knowledge of ourselves, we are going to need a plan. And we will need to dedicate some time to working on our plan. That will require honesty with ourselves and courage to do the hard things.

Following are ten Action Plans you can do that will increase your self-awareness in general but will especially increase the awareness of your emotional world. To begin, take the time to read through them and then talk with your spouse about your reactions to all ten. Each of you should choose one that you agree would be a good starting point—any that you feel comfortable beginning with. Be sure to use the feelings chart in chapter 2 as you work on the Action Plans, as this will help you name the feelings. Working together will make the process more rewarding. If your Self-Awareness scores were low, take the time to work through all ten Action Plans before moving on to the next set of Action Plans.

Action Plan #S1—Identify Your Basic Emotional Posture When Stressed

We've talked about our different options when it comes to our BEP. Some of us, when stressed, have a basic emotional posture of being angry and irritable much of the time. Others may approach life from a fearful, anxious posture. There are also those who are more melancholic, seeing life through a generalized sadness, while others are always fighting with themselves over unresolved guilt or toxic shame. There is, of course, a general posture of joy, but that is often interpreted as being overly optimistic about everything.

Take some time now and identify what you think your basic emotional posture is when stressed about life. Choose from anger, fear, shame, or sadness.

My BEP when stressed about life is _____.

Talk with your spouse and see if they agree. If not, continue to talk together and work through your different perspectives until you are both clear on your BEP. Consider why you feel this is your BEP and why your spouse thinks this is the right choice for you. Then ask yourself the following questions and discuss your answers with your spouse. Be open as you listen to each other's perspectives.

1. How were anger, fear, shame, and depression experienced in your family when you were a child?
2. Who was the family member who personified your emotional posture the most?
3. How did you respond inwardly about this as a child? What was the primary emotion that you experienced as a child?

There is something about telling your story that begins to break the hold an emotional posture has on a person. Some of these experiences are buried so deep we are unaware of how they continue to control us. But as we begin to share our story, we will remember more and have more to share.

Hearing your story also makes a difference in how your spouse responds to you. It tends to depersonalize your behavioral tendencies when you're in the grip of your BEP. It also helps your spouse to better understand how your basic emotional posture came to be.

Now answer the following questions and discuss them together:

1. What are the behavioral tendencies you exhibit when you are caught up in your basic emotional posture?
2. How are those behaviors different from how you responded outwardly as a child? How are they the same?
3. Who besides your immediate family members influenced your tendencies to behave as you do when in your BEP?

Continue to have conversations on this issue. As you work through this Action Plan, new thoughts and insights will emerge gradually. Share them with your spouse and take the time to personally reflect on what you are learning about yourself and your emotions.

Action Plan #S2—Think about Your Feelings

It may sound strange, but in this Action Plan, you are to *think* about your *feelings*. Or, to be more precise, you are to think about what you're thinking whenever you experience a feeling. In other words, what are the internal conversations you have with yourself related to those feelings? It is never easy to define what you say to yourself when you have a particular feeling, especially one associated with your BEP.

Take Don and Pat as an example. At the end of the last chapter, we imagined how differently they might have experienced the same potentially explosive interaction they'd had if they were more self-aware. How did they arrive at that change? As they spent some time on this Action Plan, Don recognized that anger was his BEP, and Pat recognized that fear was hers. For Pat, her fearful posture often led to behavioral tendencies of defending herself with anger when she was challenged by Don's anger. But she typically started from the posture of fear.

Let's follow Don's process first. As he thought about his anger, he began with the fact that the problem wasn't that he got angry. Anger and fear are both valid emotions designed to protect us from potential danger. So rather than simply blame the outburst on "I get angry; I can't help it," he had to go deeper and think about how he felt threatened, what he was saying to himself, and how he typically behaved when he got angry. He had to think about his behavioral tendencies. And that led him to the new internal conversation he was having with himself. What were the things he was telling himself in that situation?

He started his analysis by recalling what he had said out loud to Pat when he saw her wrapping the present. He remembered that he focused on what he felt was her spending too much money on her mother. And as he continued to think about how he felt Pat favored her mother, he would quickly say those thoughts out loud, and then they would both be in a heated argument and say more hurtful things.

Whenever we get caught up in our BEP, there is always an internal dialogue going on in the background that fuels the out-of-control emotional response. Because that response is almost automatic, we have to slow the process down. And we call the slowing down part "thinking about what you are feeling." As Don slowed down, he imagined what his thoughts were about the situation, and he had the opportunity to change his internal conversation.

The internal conversation connected to anger has the element of a demand associated with it. Don was making a demand on Pat, and because it involved something that had already happened, it was unenforceable. Even if it had not already happened, any demand on another person, or even on yourself, is almost impossible to enforce. So slow down and identify that demand! That's what Don was learning to do. When a similar situation arose, he slowed himself down, then he said out loud some of the changed thoughts he had identified. As a result, he managed to keep his anger in control.

Pat had to do the same thing. Because most of her internal conversation preceded the actual encounter, she was able to identify the things she was saying to herself that created internal tension. The language of her fear would always take the form of "What if . . ." Her fear was fueled by her negative imagination, which only set her up to fulfill her negative what-ifs. She was learning to articulate what she feared was going to happen.

What she had difficulty with was seeing what her internal dialogue became when Don started to get angry. Then her what-ifs became fulfilled prophecies. She also had to identify the demands she had started to make, such as, "He shouldn't talk to me like that. After all, I do the same for his mother." That took some time and effort, but she was becoming adept at playing out the internal dialogue enough times in her mind that she was also able to say it when a similar situation arose.

If sadness is your BEP, your internal dialogue will often be similar to the language of fear. When you are feeling sad, what are you telling yourself? What do you sense you're going to lose or afraid you're going to lose? Or maybe your sadness is about something you have already lost. If that is your posture, it is likely related to losses you experienced as a child. So your thinking about the sadness may begin with something happening in the here and now, but then it will take you back to things that should have happened and didn't when you were very young, or to things that happened but shouldn't have.

Those whose BEP is shame will find that they still believe some toxic false messages that were directed at them as far back as their early childhood. Toxic shame is not a naturally developed posture. It must have been set in motion by significant adults, in particular one or both parents. And it had to begin at an early age. Think through the messages you rehearse in your mind and try to remember who gave you those messages. Check out their validity by comparing them with how God sees you. God does not shame us, even when we do something wrong. His BEP toward us is always unconditional love. That is his nature. Use God's emotional posture toward you to argue against the messages of those who have shamed you. For help on seeing God's view of you, read and reread Romans 8:31–39.

It's important that you take the time and risk talking with your spouse about your internal conversations, especially those related to your BEP.

Action Plan #S3—Give a Name to Your BEP

This is a simple Action Plan. It involves giving a name to
your BEP. If you are a woman, give it a feminine name; if
you are a man, give it a masculine name. Don't choose a
name associated with someone from your personal history,
especially one related to your BEP. Give it a neutral name,
for naming it has nothing to do with why it is your BEP. Its
purpose is something else.

Once you have named your basic emotional posture,
whether it is anger, fear, sadness, or toxic shame, practice
referring to it by that name. The act of naming something
means you are in the dominant position in relation to it. When
a parent names a child, the parent is obviously dominant
over that child. Or when you name a pet, you are in charge.
When meteorologists name a hurricane, they try to make it
seem less threatening. So when you name your BEP, you are
saying that you are now in charge of "old what's-its-name."

In addition, use the name whenever you refer to that emotion while talking with your spouse. You each need to know
the name that the other has given to their BEP. For example,
Pat named her BEP of fear "Matilda," so Don could ask Pat,
"How did you do with Matilda today?" Don named his BEP
of anger "Oliver," so Pat could say to him, "I'm not comfortable when Oliver is around. Can you send him away?" The
point is for you to be dominant over your emotions.

Action Plan #S4—Keep an Emotional Journal

Writing about our emotions helps us understand them. Harry,
a husband who struggled with understanding why he would

lose control when angry, bought a special journal in which he kept notes on his experience of anger as well as a variety of emotions. When he lost his temper with his wife, he went to his journal to "think on paper about his emotion of anger."

For example, after the last argument with his wife, he reflected on his behavior and wrote down three points he wanted to remember. His first note was, "Reacted too quickly. Must slow myself down." Then he thought some more and realized he "attributed a negative connotation to what she said without checking her words for accuracy." Third, he wrote, "Need to share this with her and apologize." You will note that he did not write anything about what the argument was about. He understood that the argument wasn't about the facts. It was over their different interpretations of the facts.

Harry didn't view the journal as a means of keeping a record of his wife's emotions. It was a tool to help him understand his own emotions. There was a section where he did keep some notes on his wife, but it was in response to my explaining to him about how our faces express the universal language of emotions, as we mentioned in chapter 2. I told him to monitor his wife's face, and when he saw a look he didn't understand, he was to ask her what she was feeling at that moment. He was then to add to his journal a description of that look and the identified emotion. He reviewed his journal each evening, and in that way he became more fluent in the language of emotions.

He also started a third section in his journal, a "feeling log" of his own emotions throughout the day. Several times each day he would stop what he was doing and check in with himself regarding what he was feeling at that point in time. At first he needed to use the feeling list, but gradually he became more fluent in the language of emotions and didn't need to reference the feeling list as often. He also tried to check in with himself at the end of each day, noting what his predominant mood was during that day. Obviously, he was very serious about becoming aware of his emotions. This Action Plan doesn't need to be that intense. But there will be additional uses for a journal in some of the later Action Plans, so get a good one and put it to use.

Action Plan #S5—Identify Your Emotional Buttons

Who pushes your buttons the most? Your spouse? One of your kids? What typically is happening when it feels like someone is pushing one of your buttons? Everybody has emotional sore spots. And they are called *buttons* because it is all too easy for someone else to push them. This is especially true for how our significant others, and in particular our spouse, can set us off.

When someone's button is pushed, they are suddenly overwhelmed by negative emotions, especially defensive anger. For example, Mary would feel like exploding with rage every time her husband said to her, "Here, let me do that for you." He was baffled by her anger, thinking he was only trying to be helpful. They would often end up in what seemed to be childish arguments about his efforts to help her with certain things. After Mary's last explosion, she finally decided that her husband simply had no idea about why his words set her off. In fact, she didn't understand her reaction either. Obviously, something else was going on. He was touching a raw nerve that was tied to something painful in her past. Our buttons always have a history.

Mary spent some time thinking about her childish rage over her husband's efforts to be helpful and gradually began to realize that she was reacting to something her mother had always done to her when she was little. It seemed so obvious now, but Mary had never made the connection before. She and her husband talked about how whenever she would start a project, her mother would just take it over and finish it for her. As she began to realize this, she also started to remember the feelings she'd had in reaction to her mother's similar words.

Mary grew up feeling she was incompetent since her mother apparently saw her as always needing help. She didn't remember ever getting angry outwardly with her mother, but she remembers feeling hurt and frustrated as a child. She realized that when her husband said what he did, it felt similar to what her mother used to do, and all her stored-up anger instantly came out at him. Now, though, instead of getting angry with him, she was beginning to see that her reaction was tied to one of her buttons that had been fixed in place by her mother very early in her life.

Our buttons are typically connected to very young parts of ourselves, and their mechanisms are stored in the sub-conscious part of our mind. The subconscious mind is like the hard drive of a computer, with the programming pretty well set by the time we are six or seven years old. In itself, our subconscious is emotionless, but it is where all of our individual "programs" are stored. It is outside the realm of our awareness—our conscious mind—so its contents need to be identified and then brought into the conscious mind, where we can gradually reprogram the subconscious.

The other thing about the subconscious mind is that it is very quick—lightning fast. That's why when one of our buttons is pushed, we feel so out of control. But since the subconscious is still a part of us, we can work to better understand the roots of our vulnerable emotional spots and make some changes that will help us feel more grown-up. Here's a road map for how to reprogram your emotional buttons:

1. Talk with your spouse about what you think your buttons are. Listen to what your spouse thinks. In doing this, you bring the mechanism of the button out into the open—into the conscious zone.

2. Trace back in your memory earlier experiences of reacting, or wanting to react, as if someone had pushed your button. How far back can you remember?

3. Identify the primary person who made that vulnerable spot so raw and placed it into your emotional programming.

4. Seek to understand what was broken in that person's life that caused them to act as they did.

5. Bring that child part of yourself into the present and talk with your young self in your imagination. Continue the conversation verbally with your spouse about the process. Think of it as comforting that young part of you that has been hurt so it can be released to become part of the grown-up you.

Action Plan #S6—Pay Attention to the Physical Side of Your Emotions

In the seventeenth century, René Descartes, in his two works *The Passions of the Soul* and *The Description of the Human*

Body, suggested that the body works like a machine, that it has material properties. He said the mind, on the other hand, is nonmaterial and therefore does not follow the laws of nature. He defined the body and mind as two very different entities that may interact in some small way but are basically distinctly different from each other. His dualistic view of mind and body allowed for some excellent research on the human body over the centuries, but it also led to a separation that limited the understanding of the mind's effect on the body, and vice versa.

Today, neuroscientists clearly believe that mind and body work together intimately. I believe that God made us an integrated whole, not segregated parts. Therefore, whenever you feel an emotion, not only do you experience it in your mind, but you also feel it in your body even before you are aware of feeling it. To understand this point, try a simple experiment. Close your eyes and imagine a situation in which you would experience fear. Picture in your mind the scene as literally as possible. For example, if you are afraid of heights, imagine standing on the edge of a high cliff. Or if you can't stand closed-in places, imagine being alone in an elevator stuck between floors.

Stay with the scene for as long as you can and then stop. Open your eyes and reorient yourself to where you are, then pay attention to your body. What happened to your heart rate? Did your breathing change? Could you feel your muscles tightening? How did your stomach respond? In that experiment, most people experience physical reactions as well as a real emotion, even though the situation was only imagined. You can do the same with anger, sadness, and shame, as well as joy. Think of a joyful experience and notice the difference in what you experience physically. You are training yourself to become more aware of how your body anticipates an emotion.

Practice recalling different emotional situations you've experienced until you are able to connect the emotion to the physical reaction. Picture in your mind as many details as possible in each situation. The goal is to become increasingly aware of the emotion physically. The more you practice, the more quickly you will be able to identify an emotion even before you are aware of feeling it.

Action Plan #S7—Don't Judge Your Feelings

It's important to understand that there are no good emotions and no bad emotions. As some people accurately say, "Emotions just are." Many of us have been taught that anger is a bad emotion. In a way, that can seem to be true, but God also experiences anger, so how can it always be bad? Some people hedge around God being angry by calling it "righteous indignation." But it is still anger. The apostle Paul tells us to "be angry, and do not sin" (Eph. 4:26 NKJV). So there are ways that anger leads us to sin and ways that it does not. Therefore anger must also be said to have a good side.

One positive part of anger is that it is designed to protect us. Anger can also be good when it leads us to protest injustices or gives us creative energy, among other things. But it's confusing if we try to define what's good and what's not good about anger. It's better to see anger as an emotional signal. Its "goodness" or "badness" is reflected in how we behave when we are angry.

The same is true of fear. Sometimes it is good to be afraid. If we are being threatened in some way, it might be a good thing that fear motivates us to either freeze or run away. But if we live constantly worried, anxious, and fearful, our fear has led us into bad behavior. We are not meant to live with constant worry or anxiety.

How can sadness be good? Isn't it the same as depression? Not really. Sadness is a part of grieving, and it helps us process our losses. There's movement to sadness. It's good when it reminds us of the losses we have experienced, especially those yet to be grieved. Depression is like being stuck in sadness. There's no movement to it.

Toxic shame is always bad simply because it is toxic. We could make the same distinction by calling the bad use of anger or fear *toxic anger* and *toxic fear*, but we usually don't make that distinction.

For the purpose of this Action Plan, it is more accurate to think of our emotions as neither good nor bad; it's what we do with them that is the problem. So it is productive in our journey toward self-awareness to look at what our behavioral tendencies are and to judge them and not the emotion itself.

For example, what if we are angry because a student at our son's school is picking on our son? We'll assume that our anger is neutral, and at first it only energizes us to take some action. So we go see the principal. Because we are so upset, we start yelling and telling him how terribly he is running the school and how we're tempted to take our son out of it, and how can he call himself an educator if he allows this kind of behavior? If we are unaware that anger is our behavioral tendency, it very easily could become a counterproductive reaction, and that kind of behavior with anger is always bad.

But what if our anger motivates us to make an appointment with the principal and calmly tell him our concerns? We listen as he tells us some of the background of what's going on in the other kid's life and how the administration is aware of what he is doing. He then describes what actions they are taking to work with the bullying kid and to protect our son and others. We have a productive conversation, and he promises to continue to monitor the situation. Obviously, that is a good outcome, and therefore our neutral experience of being angry led us to act in a caring and productive way. Our behavior in response to our anger was good.

Identify your behavioral tendencies with each of the four emotions. Then focus especially on either anger or fear and describe your impulsive behavioral tendencies. What gets triggered in you that leads to the impulsive response? Write out behaviors that are in line with how you want to behave in relation to your BEP, then talk together with your spouse about them. In your discussion, make sure you don't overlook talking about your basic emotional posture. Make a commitment to helping each other work toward consistent change.

Action Plan #S8—Become Observant of the Use of Emotions in the Media

There are myriad examples of the behavioral expressions of emotions all around us. You cannot watch a TV program without observing different emotions being expressed either openly or covertly. The behavioral responses to the emotion make it clear what emotion is being expressed—what the writers want the actors to express and the viewers to feel. Make it a game—as you and your spouse watch a TV program, see who can observe an emotion first. Comment on the behaviors that follow the emotion or clearly express the emotion. Have fun with it together. Then write in your emotion journal what you observed.

Do the same when you watch a movie in a theater, except be quiet about your observations until afterward when you discuss the movie. Music is also an expression of emotions, and it is designed to stir up feelings inside the listener. When you hear a favorite piece of music, think about what emotions are being stirred in you.

If you have a favorite author, ask yourself why they are your favorite. How does this author guide you into and through the land of emotions? Great writers know how to play on our emotions as we read. They write to create a mood, to take us someplace we haven't been, to let us experience the other ways people live. They do that by tapping into our emotions.

Art is like a book or a piece of music in that the artist is also trying to create a mood or a feeling. Can you express what mood or feeling is being stirred up in you as you observe any piece of art? How about in some of your old photos? What emotions are expressed in the photo?

Whenever one of these formats grabs your attention, take a close look at why. Odds are the reason is emotional.

Action Plan #S9—Don't Avoid Being Uncomfortable

The path of greater self-awareness is not an easy one. It may be the most difficult part of our journey, for it asks that we be more aware of ourselves. And for each of us, it is not a comfortable process to see ourselves as we really are. For some time we have been working at avoiding painful issues and covering up our emotions, but now we are called to face reality and work through many things we'd rather overlook. And to do that, we are going to confront our discomfort with certain feelings and experiences.

To understand this is to understand how Eskimos and polar bears interact. Barry Lopez describes this in his book *Arctic Dreams*. To the Eskimo, the polar bear is a feared and extremely dangerous enemy, much like we might view the emotion at the core of our BEP or even emotions in general. In the Eskimo culture, a young person entering adulthood had to literally confront the polar bear. Lopez says, "To encounter the bear, to meet it with your whole life, was to grapple with something personal. . . . If you were successful you found something irreducible within yourself, like a seed. To walk away was to be alive, utterly. . . . It was to touch the bear. It was a gift from the bear."[1] A young person literally had to touch the bear and survive. Success meant that youth was an adult. The Eskimos call it "the gift from the bear."

In the same way, we will be gifted when we deal with the uncomfortable emotions in our lives—not those in another person, but the raw, pure, and often scary emotions in each of us. Leaning into those uncomfortable emotions is like touching the bear.

At some point during the process of becoming more self-aware, especially as you look at your behavioral tendencies, it will feel like you are being called upon to "touch the bear." What feelings do you try your best to avoid? Why do you think you want to avoid them? (Think deeper than just saying they are uncomfortable.) For example, some of us will do everything in our power to avoid feeling down. We were taught as children that sad feelings are to be avoided at all costs. The message might not have been clear and direct, but we got it!

There are also those who seek to avoid any joyful or positive feelings. They have found that too much joy suddenly snaps them into a painful down mood. So they keep all emotions on an even keel. Others have spent a lifetime ignoring the land of emotions, hoping that the painful ones will go away. Then they find that the emotions did not go away but have a tendency to suddenly resurface when least expected.

The important task associated with this Action Plan is to allow for and face the discomfort related to certain emotions, feelings, and moods. You will find that when you stay with the process, the discomfort will ease and you will learn some important things about yourself in the process. You will have experienced "the gift from the bear."

Action Plan #S10—Describe in Detail How You Change When under Stress

What's good about stress? Although a certain level of stress may motivate a person to persevere in an important task, stress is increasingly being blamed for all kinds of issues from depression to a compromised immune system, which leads to many terminal illnesses. That's why it's so important that we understand our personal warning systems about stress before our stress levels are out of control. We want to understand the early signs of what goes on in our bodies and minds when stress starts building—the stress may just be around the corner, but before long, it's right there in our faces.

Our bodies and our minds will tell us when we are going to be under too much stress. Increased anxiety is a warning signal, as is an upset stomach. Sometimes it takes a canker sore in our mouth or increased back pain to tell us we are pushing too hard. Fatigue that says, "I can't, but I have no other choice" is a clear signal of too much stress. The goal of this Action Plan is to clearly identify the early personal signals that indicate stress is building up—signals we often push aside as we press forward.

What does your body tell you? What are some of the things you say to yourself that indicate your stress levels are too high? Talk with your spouse about this.

It's important that you support and encourage each other on the journey into greater emotional self-awareness. Don't let up, and don't expect the journey to be accomplished overnight. It will take a lifetime to know yourself, for after all, you are a complex human being. But be assured that the journey of increasing self-awareness is worth it all. Yet there is also more to come. As we become more and more aware in the land of emotions, we can grow in our ability to manage these emotions, feelings, and moods.

M—Managing Your Emotions

As we become more aware of our emotions, we will find that we need to increasingly learn how to manage them. We no longer can allow our emotions to manage us. Awareness comes first, for we cannot effectively manage what we are not aware of.

You will soon recognize that becoming more aware of your emotions is not an easy task. And you will quickly find out the more emotions you are aware of, the more you need added skills in order to manage them.

The Failure of Our Coping Strategies

It's tempting to think that developing some coping strategies seems like an easier path. Coping doesn't require as much self-awareness or self-discipline as managing our emotions.

It bypasses the necessity to manage what we do allow ourselves to feel.

Our coping strategies may include things like counting to ten when angry. But often by the time we get to two or three, we've already lost it. Or we try walking away and disengaging, which doesn't have a very satisfying ending. It only leads to more disconnection in our marriage relationship. And how many times have we vowed to ourselves that "next time it will be different," only to repeat the frustrating and hurtful behaviors again and again? We may try to use positive affirmations, or simply give up and walk on eggshells to avoid certain subjects.

Although it is seldom done purposely, eventually most couples will fall into the trap of either one or both spouses needing to be right. That behavior never works. Even when one spouse "wins" the argument and is proven to be right, they never really win, for the loser will, consciously or unconsciously, get even at some point. It's hard to accept that the objective reality of who's right and who's wrong is not that important in a marriage relationship.

Another failing tactic we attempt is to become more controlling. Some may even think that control is a basic emotional posture, but control is not an emotion. Although it is motivated by either fear or anger, trying to control the spouse isn't considered an emotional posture but rather is an intensification of it.

We may try hard to be more in control of ourselves simply to find that, at best, doing so only works occasionally or to a certain point. More often, our efforts at control take the form of more and more subtle attempts to control our spouse. We may try to gain more control by accusing our spouse of being controlling. But attempts at control, whether of ourselves or our spouse, always meet with resistance. That's part of human nature. Even when we are trying to stay in control of our own behavior, at some level we will fight our own efforts. And when we try to control our spouse, it's guaranteed they will find some way to resist.

There was a time when the accepted strategy to use with issues of anger was to "let it all out," or what is commonly called "venting." Some years ago, this was the rage among many management groups. Studies done years later clearly made the point that rather than decreasing a person's anger, venting actually increased it. Venting was Don's, Pat's, and Kimberly's method of choice when they experienced anger. They were experienced venters. Unfortunately, unless we learn to manage our anger, we all become venters. It's part of human nature to do more of the same thing to try to fix something, even though nothing ever changes.

One particularly destructive tactic is for one or both spouses to withdraw from the battle. Why is it so destructive? Because we get married hoping to build a meaningful and satisfying connected relationship. Withdrawal is movement in the opposite direction—away from connection and relationship. Whatever connection was there before is weakened by withdrawal. Eventually it feels like the connection is held together with only a thin thread. And that's probably why so many marriages end up with spouses feeling as if they have a sort of brother-sister relationship, or they simply head in the direction of divorce. These couples have over time grown apart to the point that they are almost strangers to each other.

These failing strategies are often developed as a way to block our destructive behavioral tendencies and impulsiveness, especially when it comes to the expression of anger and fear. Many of the negative things we experience in our marriage are due to one or both of us acting impulsively in anger or in fear. The healthier choice is to learn how to manage the expression of our negative emotions, especially anger and fear. The emotions of sadness and shame also need to be managed, as they can affect our marriage relationship in negative ways as well.

It All Starts with the Amygdala

Managing our emotions is a matter of resolving the battle between our emotional brain and our reasoning brain and somehow calling a truce—or better yet, finding balance. Balance will only occur if we engage both parts of the brain, and to do that, we need to understand why there is a battle.

The problem begins because our emotional brain is always activated before the reasoning brain is brought into the picture. That's why without an awareness of what we are experiencing emotionally, our reasoning brain doesn't stand a chance to have any influence until sometime after the fact, maybe even long after the fact.

When we are overwhelmed with an emotion, our amygdala is in control. The amygdala is small, about the size of an almond. But it is a powerful part of our limbic system, which is the seat of our emotions and is located in the middle part of the brain. The limbic system also operates outside of our conscious control.

The amygdala is our warning system. It's watching as our spouse quickly loses emotional control, and it communicates to the thalamus, another part of the limbic system, that our spouse is becoming overwhelmed by their anger. It's like that robot in *Lost in Space* that flaps its arms and says, "Danger! Danger! Danger!" The amygdala is the source of our fight, flight, or freeze reaction to what is being perceived as a threat to our safety.

The thalamus relays the message to, among other parts of the brain, the basal ganglia, which directs our body movements. And it tells us to watch out and move away or press forward and make a point. Other parts of the limbic system quickly rank the importance of what is going on, giving permission to the pituitary gland to release the needed chemicals into our system. The pituitary may release calming chemicals like endorphins or oxytocin. More likely, it will release stress hormones such as histamines, adrenaline, and cortisol, which prepare us to run, fight, or freeze.

Whenever a couple gets into an argument, they are beginning a dance with their individual amygdalae. This dance creates cycles of behaviors. For Don and Pat, Pat is on a fear alert when she hears Don come home. Her amygdala is preparing her for whatever might come next.

Sure enough, when Don sees what Pat is doing, his amygdala tells him there is financial danger, as well as a sense of a loss of control of the situation. He experiences unfairness danger, loss-of-control danger, and other potential dangers. His basic emotional posture is anger, so as he listens to Pat, his brain is pouring the stress hormones into his system. He is instantly ready to amp up the conversation for a fight.

Pat's fear has also released stress hormones into her system, but she can't run away. So her fear instantly turns into anger, and as Don amps up his anger, she's now right there along with him. They go at it with each other until Don withdraws from the conversation as Pat throws her final angry volley at him. Neither one of them is able to access their reasoning brain until later, after they brood over what happened. Then maybe one of them will bring reason into the process. But by that time, the hurts have already been firmly planted in each of them.

All the interactions within our brains take place in microseconds. As a result, because Don and Pat have yet to develop the ability to manage their emotional brain, they are out of control and their actions are based on history—previous arguments and impulse. To begin to change, at least one of the spouses needs to break the cycle. To do this, they not only need for their interaction to slow down; they need to develop the skills of this second competency of SMART Love—the ability to manage their emotions. When we begin to manage what we experience emotionally, it gives the reasoning brain a chance to provide a balance to the emotional brain.

When the skills of managing the emotional brain are developed, in a microsecond, information is transferred to the prefrontal cortex of the brain. This is part of the gray matter that covers the brain, and the whole gray part is called the neocortex. The part of the neocortex that is behind the forehead and just above the eyes is called the prefrontal cortex. This makes us aware of who we are, makes executive-type decisions for our lives, and relates to motivation and finding meaning in life. It is also part of our conscious brain, so that when information is sent to the prefrontal cortex, we are aware of it and have choices to make. Basically, we have opportunities for emotional management by allowing the reasoning brain to be involved.

When there is time for the information to be sent to the prefrontal cortex, it allows us to experience mental clarity and gives us the opportunity to access the energy that will keep us on a healthier track. That doesn't mean we won't still blow it emotionally at times, but slowing down does allow us to consciously act on the basis of our previously shared values. This positive outcome is what SMART Love is all about—it is based on our growing ability to manage our emotions.

Emotions in the Bible

The God of the Bible is an emotional God, and since he created us as emotional beings, he models for us how to manage emotions. In the Old Testament, we see him experience anger at Israel for worshiping other gods, but he is also long-suffering based on the fact that he can manage that emotion perfectly. He was justifiably angry because humankind, his special part of creation, continually sinned. And he was angry with the people of Israel, who rejected him as well as his love for them.

There are also examples of God experiencing sadness. He says in Hosea 11:8, "Oh, how can I give you up, Israel? How can I let you go? . . . My heart is torn within me, and my compassion overflows." He grieves over the loss of his relationship with his people. He doesn't experience surprise, for he is omniscient, nor does he experience shame or fear, for he is omnipotent and only acts in justice and mercy. His joy can be seen in his response to creation, when he said it was all "very good."

The Bible is full of admonitions regarding managing our emotions. Take anger, for instance. Paul writes in Ephesians

4:26–27, "'Don't sin by letting anger control you.' Don't let the sun go down while you are still angry, for anger gives a foothold to the devil." He adds in Romans 12:19, "Dear friends, never take revenge. Leave that to the righteous anger of God." And in Colossians 3:8, he says it is "time to get rid of anger, rage, malicious behavior." James adds his advice in James 1:19: "You must all be quick to listen, slow to speak, and slow to get angry." In other words, manage your anger.

The Bible is just as clear when it comes to fear. Hebrews 13:6 tells us, "We can say with confidence, 'The LORD is my helper, so I will have no fear. What can mere people do to me?'" In Luke 12:4, Jesus tells the crowd of people following him, "Dear friends, don't be afraid of those who want to kill your body; they cannot do any more to you after that." The apostle Paul affirms that he is "convinced that nothing can ever separate us from God's love. Neither death nor life, neither angels nor demons, neither our fears for today nor our worries about tomorrow" (Rom. 8:38). And he reminds his student Timothy that "God has not given us a spirit of fear and timidity, but of power, love, and self-discipline" (2 Tim. 1:7).

What about shame and guilt? King David said, "Finally, I confessed all my sins to you and stopped trying to hide my guilt. I said to myself, 'I will confess my rebellion to the LORD.' And you forgave me! All my guilt is gone" (Ps. 32:5). Of course, he was talking about genuine guilt and shame, not the toxic form of shame. Paul adds, "You may believe there's nothing wrong with what you are doing, but keep it between yourself and God. Blessed are those who don't feel guilty for doing something they have decided is right" (Rom. 14:22).

When it comes to either toxic shame or genuine shame, the writer to the Hebrews reminds us, "Since we have a great High Priest who rules over God's house, let us go right into the presence of God with sincere hearts fully trusting him. For our guilty consciences have been sprinkled with Christ's blood to make us clean" (Heb. 10:21–22). And the apostle John makes it very clear that "even if we feel guilty, God is greater than our feelings, and he knows everything" (1 John 3:20), which implies he really knows when we only "feel guilty" and are not really guilty of doing something wrong.

And then there's sadness. King David writes, "I am dying from grief; my years are shortened by sadness" (Ps. 31:10). What he says is true, for unfinished grieving and sadness do shorten our lives. But sadness in grief is essential, for Solomon says, "Sorrow is better than laughter, for sadness has a refining influence on us" (Eccles. 7:3). There is a place for sadness in grieving, but it is not meant to be our basic emotional posture. If it is, then we must get to the roots of the unfinished grieving and get released from being stuck in sadness. Sometimes it takes a Christian counselor, a pastor, or a trusted friend to guide those stuck in their sadness, for eventually sadness becomes depression.

Just a quick note on joy as a core emotion. Paul instructs us to "always be full of joy in the Lord. I say it again—rejoice!" (Phil. 4:4). And Peter tells us to "be truly glad. There is wonderful joy ahead, even though you must endure many trials for a little while" (1 Pet. 1:6).

The Bible's approach to each of these emotions, with the exception of joy, is that they are to be managed. We are not to let them control us. So as we move on to lay out a plan of action, think first about which of the four negative emotions is easiest for you to manage, and which is the most difficult. The latter is probably your basic emotional posture. Keep that in mind as we look at what we can do to develop the ability to manage all four emotions.

The Goal in Managing Your Emotions

Obviously, our goal is not to suppress our emotions but to manage them in such a way as to create a balance between our two brains. When you actively choose how you are going to act when you feel a certain emotion, you create a growing sense of integrity, comfort, and fairness in your marriage. You will also experience a greater degree of mutual respect.

So how do you get started? If you have worked through the first competency of SMART Love, which is being aware of your emotions, you've already laid the groundwork for developing this competency.

As we continue to do the awareness Action Plans, we are becoming more attentive to the fact that our thought patterns are just that—they are thoughts about reality but do not accurately describe reality. Your spouse is not creating the emotions you are feeling; your emotions come from what you are telling yourself about what your spouse is saying or doing. It's easy to forget that your thoughts create and stir up your emotions.[1] Remind yourself, "I am having these thoughts, and they are at the root of what I'm feeling. My spouse is not making me feel this way."

Jerry, the husband of the explosive Kimberly, had as his BEP the emotion of fear. Gradually he worked on identifying the thoughts that led him into this posture. For example, when Kimberly would begin to amp up her anger, Jerry would suddenly feel like he was paralyzed. Later, he could recall some of his thoughts: *What if I say something I can't back up? What if I make it worse? I'm better off just keeping my mouth shut—at least I don't make it worse. Why can't she calm down? My heart is racing. I don't agree, but I'll keep my mouth shut and just get out of here.*

As we talked together, he saw the fear in his "what-ifs" and that his silence only made things worse. So he made a commitment to Kimberly and me that the next time they had an argument, he would say what he wanted but had always been afraid to say. Later they described what happened. As Kimberly was getting more agitated, he suddenly blurted out, "I don't agree!" Both of them were so surprised that there was a long moment of silence, and then they started to laugh. When they stopped laughing, they started talking. It was almost as if Jerry had broken free, for he was able to talk with Kimberly about the subject, and she didn't get upset. In fact, she was so pleased that he had finally said something, they talked for almost an hour as they resolved that issue and several others.

As Jerry identified how his internal commentary on what Kimberly was saying and doing was at the root of his fears, he was able to face them. As he did, his fears grew smaller and more manageable. More and more he was able to accept his inner dialogue as just that—thoughts about reality. He found he had more choices in how to respond to Kimberly, and she in turn was beginning to manage her anger more effectively.

Jerry and Kimberly also found that as they grew in their ability to manage their emotions, there was a greater openness in their relationship regarding what they were thinking and experiencing together. They experienced a genuine openness based on a mutual sense of being responsible to each other. And surprisingly to each of them, they were becoming more optimistic about their future together.

As they were better able to manage their emotions, they found that they wanted to spend more time together. Since Jerry's fear was more under control, he could be more affectionate with Kimberly. And for the first time, he was beginning to be more engaged with Kimberly's other emotional responses to him.

Now, let's build on your previous Action Plans. In the next chapter you'll find ten more Action Plans designed to help you build your skills and become more comfortable in managing your emotions.

Managing Your Emotions
Action Plans

We cannot manage our emotions unless we are growing in our ability to be more aware of them. The more aware we are of our feelings, the more we can increase our ability to manage what we feel. Managing what we feel goes beyond our ability to control what we feel and do as a result.

The apostle Paul, in Galatians 5:22–23, tells us that "the Holy Spirit produces this kind of fruit in our lives: love, joy, peace, patience, kindness, goodness, faithfulness, gentleness, and self-control." You've already tried to control your negative emotional responses and found that it seldom works. You think you need more of the fruit of the Spirit, especially self-control.

But self-control is different from managing our emotions. While managing our emotions does require a degree of self-control, it goes beyond that to realizing we have behavioral choices we can make. We *can* choose to respond to a negative emotion in a constructive way.

When we act impulsively, our reaction is always preceded by some subtle signals that warn us we are beginning to lose it. We begin to develop the skills of managing our emotions when we learn to pay attention to the warning signals and realize we can make better behavioral choices. So part of managing our emotions is learning to pay attention to the warning signals early in the process.

The more you understand the internal dialogue that is at the root of any negative emotion, the more you will be able to choose how you will respond. You will also find that the earlier you recognize these signals, the more power you will have to make better choices in how you behave.

Continue to work on the Self-Awareness Action Plans you started in chapter 5, and gradually add and work on the Action Plans that follow.

Action Plan #M1—Manage Anger

For most people, anger is the most difficult emotion to manage. This six-step plan will help you slow down and learn how to manage that explosive emotion.

1. Take five! Say something like, "I need a minute" or "Give me a minute, please." Or call a time-out for five minutes. Be careful you don't fall into the pattern of calling a time-out and then never coming back to the subject at hand.

2. During that break, allow your body to discharge the energy associated with the anger. You've already started doing that by temporarily stopping the interaction. Now take some slow, deep breaths. Breathe in slowly and exhale slowly four or five times. Get some oxygen to your brain. As you're breathing deeply, remind yourself that you want to act in love.

3. Memorize Ephesians 4:31–32 so you can repeat it in your mind. "Get rid of all bitterness, rage, anger, harsh words, and slander, as well as all types of evil behavior. Instead, be kind to each other, tenderhearted, forgiving one another, just as God through Christ has forgiven you." Doing this will begin to change your thoughts.

4. Listen to your anger. What is at stake here for you? What is being threatened for you? Anger is typically related to a demand we can't enforce. Try to identify the demand you are making in this situation that you really can't enforce.

5. Consider yourself to be part of the problem. Ask yourself, *What am I doing or saying that is adding to the tension? What am I thinking or telling myself that is fueling the anger?*

6. When the break is over, if nothing has changed, ask for a "do-over." That means you negate what has just happened and start the conversation over from the beginning.

Remember, the goal is to manage the emotion of anger. It is not to repress or suppress it. There is a reason you are angry. But as you implement this six-step process, you will find your reason often has nothing to do with what is going on in the here and now.

Action Plan #M2—Manage Fear and Anxiety

In some situations, fear is going to be a pervasive feeling, and it can be very difficult to manage. Here is a four-step plan to help you manage the emotion of fear.

1. Start by putting what you fear into words and say it out loud. Say it to your spouse. Tell them you are feeling either fearful or anxious right now. The difference between fear and anxiety is that I can identify what I fear, but when I am feeling anxious, it is experienced as a generalized state that has no focus. So if your spouse asks, "What are you afraid of?" if it is fear, you will be able to answer. But if they ask, "Why are you feeling anxious?" your answer usually will be something like, "I don't really know exactly. I just have this feeling of dread." So the first step is to say out loud what you are feeling.

2. Once you have verbalized your fear and/or anxiety, it is important that your spouse be supportive. Whenever we are afraid or anxious, we need reassurance. We don't want them to say something like, "That's ridiculous. You shouldn't feel that way!" That's clearly not supportive.

   Think of a three-year-old who is afraid. He is certain there are monsters under his bed or in the closet. A wise parent doesn't say something like, "That's silly, there are no monsters there. Go to sleep!" Instead, they take the fear seriously and reassure the child there is nothing under the bed. They may get down and crawl partway under the bed or look in the closet to reassure the child. The wise parent would never minimize the child's fears or ridicule him for being afraid, for they know that only adds to the fear. What's true with a child is equally true for any adult experiencing fear or anxiety!

3. If it is true that what we need from our spouse is re-assurance, then what we are asking for is a form of being soothed. In addition, we need to learn how to self-soothe. Self-soothing can be thought of as calming our amygdala. Creating the sense that there is no emergency or threat can be calming. You can do this by going for a walk, brewing a cup of hot tea, or petting your dog. Some of us are soothed by the taste of chocolate—it helps us to calm down. Rubbing the tops of your thighs is also a soothing action, as is the sensation of rocking. We need the soothing offered by our spouse, but fortunately, we also can learn to self-soothe.

4. If your spouse is reassuring and soothing, show your appreciation. Even if you needed more than they were able to give, appreciate what they do give you.

Action Plan #M3—Plan Ways to Exit a Down Mood

Our emotions can create moods within us. Emotions are more intense and usually don't last over a long period of time. Moods are less intense but are more long lasting. They can come and take residence within us. We have up moods, where we feel like everything is going great. We love having up moods. In our marriage, when we have an up mood, it is likely to also lift the mood of our spouse. On the other hand, our spouse may try to pour cold water on our up mood and knock us into a down mood, but fortunately, down moods aren't as easily transferred. If we're in a down mood, our spouse will pick up on it but not join in it. They just generally check us out and then leave us alone.

We can usually catch on rather easily to the mood of our spouse. When a husband comes home, his wife will typically judge his mood by a look on his face, by the tone of his voice, and maybe even through her intuition. A husband can sometimes identify the mood of his wife upon her arrival at home as well, but her mood usually has to be pretty obvious for the husband to pick it up. Generally speaking, moods are hard to hide. And they go beyond just being optimistic or pessimistic.

Moods tend to linger because they affect our perceptions by hooking into our negative memories. When we are in a good mood, we tend to see things in a more upbeat way and recall the good parts of a memory. Because of the distortion of perceptions, bad moods may perpetuate themselves more because they are stressful and cause the brain to release stress hormones, which are hard for the body to reabsorb. So the mood lingers unless we have a strategy.

Creating a plan for exiting down moods will therefore involve shifting our focus. Instead of focusing on the negative aspects of a situation, choose to focus on the positives. Instead of focusing on the negative emotion underlying the mood, focus on the promise of God's faithfulness. Write out on a 3 x 5 card some of the passages that reassure you of God's care and recite them to yourself. Instead of focusing on the limitations, focus on the opportunities. This requires self-discipline, for your spouse cannot initiate this process. It must be something you choose to do and persist in doing. But your spouse can help by having an infectious up mood.

When you are in a down mood, you may need to stop watching the news or listening to the twenty-four-hour news station on the radio. You may even need to stop reading the newspaper, for they all thrive on bad news, which only reinforces your mood. Watch something funny on TV or go see a funny movie. Smile a lot, laugh even more. When you smile or laugh, you use muscles on your face that communicate to your emotional brain that things are improving emotionally. Try to bury yourself temporarily in something that interests you and grabs your emotions. Read something that is fun and emotionally uplifting. These things will help you detach from whatever has created your down mood and give you the freedom to see things in a better light.

Action Plan #M4—Define the War between the Emotional Brain and the Reasoning Brain

The next time the battle is raging between your emotional brain and your reasoning brain, stop what you're doing, get a piece of paper, and draw a line down the middle. On one side write what the emotional brain is telling you; on the other side, write what the reasoning brain is telling you.

Don did this in relation to his mother and his mother-in-law. The emotional side was saying things like, "Pat is so unfair. She favors her mother. Maybe she doesn't even like my mother. That really puts me in a bad spot. Why does she have to be so sneaky about it all? What's she hiding?"

His reasoning brain was saying things like, "I know Pat likes my mother. She's obviously closer to her own mother, and it is easier for her to do things with and for her mom because she lives close by. I don't know why I make this an issue. Pat has always tried to be fair about our families."

When Don looked at the two lists, he was surprised to see the difference. The distortions were mostly on the emotional brain's side of the list. It became clear to him that he needed to slow down and give his emotional brain time to get in touch with his rational brain.

Think back to a previous battle between your own two brains. Or, if there is occasion to do so, consider a current situation. Make a list of the points each side is making. Don't evaluate what is true or not; just write down your opposing thoughts.

When you have finished, look at what you wrote. Look for the ways your emotions affect your being able to think clearly. Look also for the ways your reasoning brain ignored some key emotional issues. Then share what you have written with your spouse. Remember, the goal is not to declare a "winner" but to strive for a balance between your two brains that sees the value in both sides of the argument.

Action Plan #M5—Share Emotional Experiences

This exercise is designed to tap into your emotions in a controlled way. It begins with a generalized discussion about how your day went. As you each talk about some of the things that happened during your day, listen with the ears of your emotions. When something your spouse says strikes you in a positive way emotionally, such as stirring up your own feelings or triggering a memory of a similar situation, wait until the person is finished talking. Then say the following, replacing the bracketed statements to fit your situation: "When you shared [what was said], I felt [an emotion], and it reminded me of [the memory or experience that was triggered]."

Then discuss together each of your responses to the statement. For example, a wife shared with her husband something she did that day with their kids at the park. She told him how their four-year-old daughter kept wanting to be pushed higher and higher on the swing, even to the point where Mom was starting to become a little scared. When the swing was at its farthest point from Mom as the swing-pusher, it seemed to her that it would almost stop and then drop before it swung back again. Of course, that was the part the daughter enjoyed the most.

Her husband listened as she described the event, and when she stopped he said, "When you shared how the swing would almost stop and then drop before swinging back, I first felt great joy, because it reminded me of how I loved that excitement on the swings when I was a kid. Then I felt sadness because you get to share that with the kids and I don't get those opportunities very often."

The wife responded by saying, "As you say that, I too feel sad that you don't get to share that with our kids very often. Let's plan a picnic at the park this Saturday with all of us and the kids. You can push our daughter on the swings." Both were talking about their emotions in a managed way, and it led to a plan for a family outing.

Follow this example when you are sharing about your day, about an experience one of you had, or about something another person shared with one of you. Simply use the example sentence to initiate a conversation in which your emotions are being managed.

Action Plan #M6—Define and Discuss Your Goals as a Couple

Everyone has goals. Some people won't admit to having goals or won't talk about them. In many cases they don't talk about them because they think that if they do, the goals become set in concrete and must at all costs be accomplished. Then there are others who have goals, talk about them freely, and seem to hold on to them loosely, for they are always under revision.

Couples also have goals, but they seldom talk with each other about them. Some couples' goals are simply to avoid any conflict. They are tired of the uproar and just want peace. But I've found that when couples make real, meaningful goals, it strengthens their marriage in many ways. It's also a powerful way for both parties to better manage their own emotions.

To help a couple articulate their goals, I use an intervention that is based in their imagination and is set five years in the future. Here's their assignment:

Since this is set five years in the future, you are to assume that all problems and issues have been resolved, and you now have the marriage you've always dreamed of having. Imagine I accidentally meet one of you at the mall, and I haven't seen you in four years.

In our conversation, I ask how your marriage is going. You tell me, "I now have the marriage I always dreamed of having! It's perfect!" Of course, I don't believe you, for nothing is ever perfect, so I ask you for evidence of its perfection. You make a list of all the things that, five years in the future, would result in the perfect marriage for you.

The husband and wife each do this separately. When they have finished writing out the product of their imaginings, we look together at what they have written. Contrary to what many couples typically fear, there is little difference between their two lists. The only difference is usually the order of the things they would be experiencing.

Now you and your spouse make this list, and when you have finished, you'll have the raw materials for creating meaningful goals for your marriage. Pick two or three items that are on both of your lists, and restate them as five-year goals—for example, "Five years from now, we will experience together . . ." Then pick just one of the goals. Obviously, if you are to reach that goal in five years, you will need a subset of shorter goals. So talk about what would need to happen in three years, in one year, in six months, and today to start on the road to reaching that goal. Write that down.

Your goals should build on your strengths, not your weaknesses. And they should be flexible.

Now that you have articulated some goals for your marriage, share them with your grown kids, if you have them, or with another couple you know well. Going public with your goals is one of the best ways to get support in reaching them. But don't become compulsive about your goals. If you need to adjust them along the way, do so. Just be sure to share the changes with your kids or with your couple friends.

Action Plan #M7—Spend Time Playing Together

As a couple, what do you do for fun together? Think back to when you were first married or to your time together before kids came along. What did you do for fun? It seems that once the kids arrive, family takes precedence, and rightly so. But then the fun things are family things. It is the rare couple that also focuses on the fun stuff in their own relationship. When the kids are grown, there is an interlude before the grandkids arrive, and then we have fun with them.

It could be argued that having fun together with the kids or with the grandkids is fun for a couple, but it is equally important to have fun together as a couple only, and with other couples. Sit down together and discuss what you currently do to have fun together and what things you'd like to do. Then gradually initiate some of the new ideas and keep experiencing the fun things you are already doing.

One couple plans a fun outing every month. They alternate being the planner of the outing. They do the same with their anniversary, again taking turns doing a surprise outing for them to experience together. Start simple—plan something fun for just the two of you once a month.

Action Plan #M8—Manage Your Self-Talk

Everyone talks to themselves. The question is, are you listening to yourself? Can you image how much you talk to yourself? Studies suggest that we have about 50,000 word-thoughts a day. We can talk to ourselves at a rate of up to 1,300 words per minute. That's pretty fast, especially when you realize that a good typist can type 100 words per minute, and we can only handwrite up to 31 words per minute. The average reader reads between 250 and 300 words per minute. Steve Woodmore holds the Guinness World Record for speaking at the rate of 637 words per minute. But those are all very slow compared to how fast words fly by in our thoughts!

The irony is that we seldom pay attention to the flow of our thoughts, even though they positively or negatively influence our emotions the most. Paul instructs us in 2 Corinthians 10:5 to "demolish arguments and every pretension that sets itself up against the knowledge of God, and we take captive every thought to make it obedient to Christ" (NIV). He has great insight into how our thoughts are connected to our emotions. We are to capture our thoughts and focus on those that are good for us. In Romans 12:2 he writes, "Let God transform you into a new person by changing the way you think." Our thoughts are critical in determining who we are and what we feel.

The problem with our self-talk is that we all have a proclivity to turn to the negative. For example, think about your day yesterday. Let's say that twenty different things happened to you, and nineteen of them were positive. Only one was negative. What did you ruminate on all day, and what did you focus on as you put your head on your pillow? The one negative thing, of course! That's called negative self-talk, and it will block your ability to manage your negative emotions.

Here are some negative value judgments we make about ourselves:

I am unworthy of . . .
I am worthless.
I am so stupid.

I am hopeless.

It's all my fault.

And you can probably add more to the list.

How does someone "take captive every thought"? It's probably impossible to capture *every* thought, but we can focus on those that frequently trip us up. Take a sheet of paper and make three columns. In the left-hand column, list examples of your frequent negative self-talk. For example, you might be dealing with guilt over something that happened recently. So the column might begin with the statement, "If only I hadn't said what I said. I can't believe how I hurt _____." Or you might write, "I shouldn't have yelled at my son. I could see the hurt on his face."

In the middle column, describe the emotion you feel as a result of the thoughts you wrote in the left column. You might write "guilt" for the first sentence; you might write "anger" for the second sentence. Write out several pages of negative thought statements you've made to yourself recently, then identify the emotion that you feel as you read the statement to yourself.

The third column is the key. After you have worked your way through the left column and the middle column, identifying the thoughts and the resulting emotions, you are ready to work on the right-hand column. Here you are to rewrite the statement in the left column in a way that negates the negative emotion.

You could rewrite the first statement as something like, "I sure wish I hadn't said what I did to _____. I need to apologize to her." Can you feel the difference between those two statements? For the second statement, maybe rewrite it like this: "I can't believe I yelled at my son again, knowing how sensitive he is. I'm going to talk to him and let him know how sorry I am, and that I will handle things differently with him in the future." As you read the rewritten versions of the statements, hopefully you can feel the release of the self-oriented tension that was contained in the first versions. Once you realize the difference, make the apology in person.

Use this writing exercise whenever you get caught up in negative self-talk. Try to do the three columns in your head as well. The goal is to make this change such a habit that you no longer need to do the writing exercises.

Action Plan #M9—Make a List of Your Own Shortcomings

This may feel like a self-awareness exercise, but its purpose takes it beyond self-awareness to helping you better manage the behaviors associated with your negative emotions. Take some time to reflect on where you fall short of your own or your spouse's perceived expectations. This is designed purposely to be a humbling Action Plan. One of the benefits of genuinely and humbly knowing ourselves is our willingness to become more transparent in our emotional relationship with our spouse.

For example, if one of your shortcomings is a tendency to procrastinate, even on important things, then write that on your list. Or maybe you get impatient with other adults and with your kids. Write it down. You are doing a personal inventory of as many of your shortcomings as you can. Paul instructs us to "be honest in your evaluation of yourselves" (Rom. 12:3).

Now comes the humbling part: share your list with your spouse. This is a confession time, for you are going to verbally validate with your spouse what they probably already know about you. There is value in being able to confess to each other. James tells us that when we confess, we experience healing (see James 5:16). He also reminds us to humble ourselves so that God can lift us up in honor (see James 4:10). With this Action Plan, the humbling is to lead to greater emotional transparency.

Action Plan #M10—Define and Discuss Your Personal Values

Maintaining the balance between the emotional brain and the reasoning brain requires that we act based on our values, not on our impulses. In many ways, our impulses cause us to hold our values rather loosely. Here is an exercise in identifying your values. Work on it alone, and then share the process with your spouse. It's good to clarify not only your own core beliefs and values but also your spouse's.

First, read through the list of personal values below and select the seven that are most important to you. You can each use a different-colored highlighter to mark your top seven.

Personal Values

Achievement	Duty	Initiative	Rationality
Adaptability	Efficiency	Integrity	Recognition
Ambition	Environment	Intuition	Reliability
Autonomy	Excellence	Leadership	Respect
Awareness	Fairness	Learning	Responsibility
Balance	Family	Leisure	Risk

Being the Best	Forgiveness	Meaning	Safety
Caring	Friendships	Money	Security
Comfort	Fun	Openness	Success
Commitment	Generosity	Order	Tolerance
Compassion	Growth	Patience	Trust
Competence	Harmony	Peacemaking	Truth
Cooperation	Honesty	Perseverance	Vision
Courage	Humility	Power	Wealth
Creativity	Humor	Purity	Well-Being
Dependability	Independence	Purpose	Wisdom

Once you have picked seven values, write down the three that are most important to each of you.

_____ _____ _____

_____ _____ _____

Why do you believe that these are most important to you?

What behaviors do you generally exhibit that support each value?

What behaviors do you generally exhibit that are counter to your values?

When you have finished, discuss your value list and your responses to the questions. You might want to repeat this Action Plan on a monthly basis so you can be more aware of how your values are a part of your daily decisions, especially as you work toward modifying and managing your behavioral tendencies.

A—Accountability

Being accountable to each other in a marriage is an essential part of SMART Love. One of the wisest men who ever lived, King Solomon, wrote,

> Two people are better off than one, for they can help each other succeed. If one person falls, the other can reach out and help. But someone who falls alone is in real trouble. Likewise, two people lying close together can keep each other warm. But how can one be warm alone? A person standing alone can be attacked and defeated, but two can stand back-to-back and conquer. Three are even better, for a triple-braided cord is not easily broken. (Eccles. 4:9–12)

Solomon was talking about the power of two or three being able to defend and protect one another. His words equally apply to the marriage relationship. They also call a couple to be accountable to themselves individually, to each other, and to other trusted couples. Being accountable to each other is a foundational part of feeling connected to each other—you are a team. It's a central part of SMART Love.

When we talk about accountability in marriage, we are not in any way suggesting that husbands and wives become cops or demanding tyrants toward each other. Accountability begins as a personally oriented process. We begin by holding ourselves accountable for our thoughts, feelings, and behaviors. From that solid foundation, we learn to be accountable to our spouse out of love for them. And if we're a wise couple, we go a step further and bring in a third party—other trusted couples to whom we are mutually accountable.

Personal Accountability

Being personally accountable begins with our being responsible for our thoughts, motives, and actions as adults. Being responsible in marriage is based on how much we think the success of our marriage is up to us. I've talked with many couples who believe marriage is to be a 50/50 proposition. The problem with that approach is that at some point in time one partner might decide they have to give more than 50 percent. They may have to give 60 percent, but when they do, they struggle with a sense of things being unfair. They're doing more than they bargained for.

Personal responsibility in a marriage works best when it is more like an 85/85 proposition. When both spouses are giving 85 percent, fairness ceases to be an issue. I used to say it should be 100/100, where each partner is fully responsible.

But since nothing is ever perfect, I now leave 15 percent to the unknowns in the relationship.

What is the difference between being responsible and being accountable? Responsibility relates to the things in your life and marriage over which you have control—things like your work, your thoughts, and your behaviors when you're alone. These are the areas where you first have to think and behave with integrity as a married person. Accountability goes beyond responsibility to the point of being willing to give an account of your responsibilities.

There are three parts to being personally responsible. The first requirement is to *be truthful* with each other. In our culture today, it seems like everyone lies and no one really expects otherwise. It seems okay for adults to lie, but not our kids. And our kids know when we lie. Couples also know when their spouse is lying, but unless it is a major issue, it's often overlooked.

There are basically three kinds of lies. The first are the intentional lies, when we purposely stretch the truth in order to cover up something we don't want to be held accountable for. A husband lies about where he has been when he comes home two hours late. A wife lies about how much she spent on her new shoes. Intentional lies that we don't correct are at the root of toxic shame, at least until we can numb our consciences. This kind of lie is very damaging to a marriage and, of course, undermines the ability to be trusted.

Then there are the so-called white lies, when we bend the truth so as not to hurt someone, or when we don't want to deal with a confrontational conversation. We sacrifice the truth for some kind of peace, at least until the truth eventually comes out.

Third, there are the lies of omission. These are the things that, intentionally or not, we choose to omit from the conversation. The wife thinks her husband is working late, but he's watching the game at a sports club with co-workers and tells his wife he just stopped for a beer on the way home. The game is never brought up. Similarly, she doesn't even mention the new shoes.

Being personally responsible seeks to minimize all three types of lies. Telling the truth is the foundation for trusting each other. When a lie slips into the conversation, it needs to be cleared up as quickly as possible. To do this, we need to develop the second part of being responsible, which is to *police ourselves*. We need to begin by being responsible ourselves. The goal is not to be *held* responsible; it is to *be* responsible. This means keeping track of how we are doing.

The third part of responsibility is that we always need to *look to ourselves*. It means we learn to ask this question on a regular basis: "What am I doing that contributes to the problem we are facing?" That's also being accountable to ourselves! If we need help developing this ability, it is always good to seek out someone and agree to be accountable to them as a mentor.

To choose an accountability mentor, first identify in yourself where you need some accountability. Then select someone of the same sex who seems to be more mature, both personally and spiritually. Approach this person, share the issue you need help with, and ask if they are willing to hold you accountable without being judgmental. This person also needs to be someone who is not afraid to challenge you. Then agree to meet regularly and work on a plan that leads to positive growth in the area of your concern.

Accountability depends on our willingness to be honest. John had had an affair that lasted for several months. When his wife, Ashley, discovered it, she was committed to working on restoring their marriage. They both agreed that part of that restoration involved coming to counseling. John seemed very sincere, describing the accountability group he had put together. His wife was impressed, for she was surprised at one or two of the men he had chosen. The men created a small group Bible study and continued to spend time checking in on how they were doing personally, how they were doing with their wives, and how things were going with their work.

Three years later, Ashley found evidence that John's affair had never completely ended. It had only tapered off for a while to avoid suspicion, and then he picked up where he had left off. All the while John was in his "accountability group."

This time Ashley was done. She kept saying, "I thought he was being accountable, and he not only fooled me, he fooled the other six men in his group." This was a painful picture of John appearing to be accountable, but it was only part of his deception. He had never been accountable to himself, let alone anyone else, especially Ashley. Willingness is a key component of both personal responsibility and personal accountability. John chose instead to live a life of lying, both to himself and to everyone else around him.

Couples Being Accountable to Other Couples

Couples also need to have other trusted couples in their lives to whom they are accountable. One of the strengths in our own marriage is being part of a group made up of five couples. We call ourselves "D'Tenavus," for there are ten of us. For over thirty years, we have arranged our schedules to get together for a long weekend twice a year. We all live in different parts of California, so once a year we meet in Southern California, and once a year we meet in Northern California. The amazing thing is no one has ever missed a weekend!

One of the highlights of our time together has been the silly, fun activities we have done. We've had competitions for dumb things, like when the guys dressed in grass skirts and bras and competed with each other as hula dancers, which none of us really did well. It was silly but great fun, and the pictures we each have of the competition are a wonderful reminder of that time, even though they are embarrassing when our kids ask about them. So be careful to get and keep friends with whom you can not only let your hair down but also be accountable.

The accountable part of our time together as couples is when we share what is going on in our lives, in our families, and in our marriages. Each couple takes their turn sharing, and we finish their turn by praying for them. And we have prayed for each other on a daily basis as well for thirty years. We continue to stand in accountability with each other as we've grieved the death of one of the men and the serious illnesses of several of the women. We've had other couples as close friends as well, and all of those friendships have given stability to our marriage.

The willingness of a couple to be accountable to each other is based on their mutual willingness to be personally accountable. If I am not accountable to myself, I cannot be accountable to my spouse. Being accountable to each other is following Paul's injunction in Ephesians 5:21, where he urges husbands and wives to "submit to one another out of reverence for Christ." It takes a submissive spirit in both husbands and wives for them to be accountable to each other.

This is often a challenge for the men. One of the highest predictors of marital success, identified in the research of John Gottman at the University of Washington, is when a husband honors and validates his wife's suggestions. It doesn't mean he does everything she asks, but he takes seriously and considers everything she suggests. The wife has to believe she is being taken seriously. On the other hand, if the wife takes her husband seriously, it predicts nothing. That's probably because a wife usually does value what her husband is suggesting. It's an interesting distinction. The point is, it's important that the wife knows her ideas and suggestions are valued, even when not always followed.

The reason this factor is such an important predictor of success is that men typically struggle with even hearing their wives' suggestions. A man is off to fix the problem. Men also have a wide variety of responses to their wives' suggestions, all the way from being wimps who always do what the wife says to being tyrants. Those on the extreme ends of the continuum don't give value to their wives, while those somewhere in the middle do. They are the winners, even though our culture often attaches unsavory labels to men who are willing to accept influence from their wives.

Areas of Spousal Accountability

There are at least five areas in which couples need to be accountable to each other. First is the area of their *emotional and sexual fidelity*. This is a critical and particularly sensitive area in any marriage, but one that needs to be a clear part of mutual accountability. It needs to begin with a mutual openness in the areas of temptations and moral struggles.

Think of it this way. Let's say you're a woman in a couples' Bible study, and one of the wives seems overly interested in your husband. She is just too friendly. When this kind of thing happens, wives have a special ability to pick up on it. So a wise husband needs to take it seriously when his wife calls attention to what she believes is happening. (Husbands are quite different—they seem oblivious to such things, except to enjoy the attention they are unsuspectingly receiving.)

Now what if the couple hasn't developed the willingness to be accountable to each other in this area of their marriage? The husband will probably minimize what his wife is telling him, assuming she has the courage to say something. If she does say something, he may act a little macho about it and say things like, "That's ridiculous! It's your imagination!" What happens next is that the wife's suspicion is confirmed, both to her and to the other women in the group. And then who knows where the situation ends up.

Now, in contrast, the couple who is comfortably and willingly accountable to each other has the same initial conversation. But the husband listens and begins to pay attention to what he hasn't been seeing. He talks about it with his wife, and together they come up with a set of behavioral changes that don't confront the other woman but make it clear that there is no interest on his part. He responds in a supportive and accountable way to his wife's concerns.

As a couple, we need to be comfortable talking about our temptations and weaknesses in the area of being faithful to each other. Our culture feeds a man's tendency to lust whether he wants to or not. Advertising, TV programs, and movies all celebrate the female body and are designed to stir up feelings of lust and envy. Can you as a husband talk to your wife about these issues? If you're going to willingly be accountable to each other regarding sexual issues, you need to be courageous enough to be able to talk about them in the beginning stages. Don't wait for these thoughts to go underground, so to speak, and become a major problem.

Second, couples need to be accountable regarding their *spiritual health*. One of the best ways a couple can do this is by praying together on a daily basis. We've been doing this as a couple for many years. In the early years of our marriage, I resisted the idea to the point where Jan finally gave up trying. I could pray in front of the church, with other staff, with people in my office, and even with the family. But to pray alone with Jan seemed too threatening.

But when Jan backed off, that gave me room to quit resisting and to "bite the bullet," as I often would say. Once we started praying together, we not only developed the consistency of praying every day, we also became comfortable stopping at any time and praying together about a specific issue. Several research studies have shown that when couples do spiritual things together at home on a consistent basis, their marital satisfaction improves dramatically. Things like praying together, reading the Bible together, and finding ways to serve together have the same effect of strengthening the marriage—especially the commitment to pray together as a couple.

Third, couples need to be accountable to each other regarding their *schedule*. I recently talked with a husband who was overwhelmed by the demands on his time. His wife was the loser in his conflict, as he felt he had to be available 24-7 to the demands of his boss. He and his wife both needed to become accountable to each other regarding their schedules, learning not only how to say yes but especially how to say no.

For years, when our kids were still at home and in school, Jan and I had a Friday morning ritual. My week would end late on Thursday evening, and we reserved Friday morning for just the two of us. We headed to a special restaurant on the sand at the beach for breakfast. There we would often sit for several hours after enjoying our breakfast, unwinding, but most importantly catching up with each other. Sometimes one of us had a request to do something else on a Friday morning, but our answer was always, "No, I have another commitment that can't be changed."

Fourth, couples need accountability when it comes to their *money*—how they give it, how they save it, and very importantly, how they spend it. They need to talk about whether their financial behaviors are based on their values or on impulse. One of the major conflict areas in marriage is the issue of money. In a marriage, money represents power. Whoever controls the money has the power. That's why some husbands control the money so tightly that their wives don't have a clue about how much money they have as a couple. There's no accountability, but there is a sense of power for the one who controls the money, especially when it is kept a secret from the spouse.

I've talked with wives who have no idea what their husband makes, how much money they have in reserve, or, if they do have various accounts, what is in them. The wife feels totally powerless, especially if she and her husband are getting up in years. I've also talked with husbands who can't understand why their wife runs up the credit cards so high every month. I remind the husband that this might reflect a common situation if he doesn't really show any positive attention to the wife. Her spending at least gets some attention from him, even though it is negative attention and typically causes a major argument.

Your spending reveals your values to yourself and your spouse. Go back to Action Plan #M10 at the end of the last chapter, and discuss together how your top three values impact the way you handle your money. We all too often speak of our values but then contradict them with our behaviors. Make adjustments to your behaviors to make certain they are in accord with your stated values.

Fifth, if you have children, you as a couple need to be accountable to each other regarding *how you are parenting.* We went through a tough time with one of our kids and struggled with the issue of being kind and firm at the same time. When one of us was trying to be kind and understanding, the other was trying to be strong and firm. Occasionally we would switch roles—the kind parent tried being strong and firm, and the firm parent was suddenly filled with kindness. We missed the goal of being kind and firm at the same time. It isn't easy!

Being accountable as parents means we can talk together openly about what we see each other doing or not doing and encourage each other in the goal of being both kind and firm. There are a variety of effective parenting approaches, and they each have something to offer. To be effective, we need to know how we were parented and how our spouse was parented, for we all start either imitating or reacting against what we experienced. Effective parenting always requires that we be on the same page with our spouse, and that almost always means a continuing sense of openness and accountability with each other.

Summary

So what have we said about accountability? Remember, accountability in your marriage relationship always comes from within. It's not that we are being held accountable; it's that we willingly choose to be accountable. Our accountability is based on being truthful with ourselves and with our spouse. It's not something we try for a while; it's an integral and ongoing part of SMART Love.

There is also a sense that accountability has to be planned. Developing rituals with each other or with other trusted couples that keep us accountable requires a plan. It doesn't just happen. But we need to hold each other accountable in the context of loving behavior.

It's good also to have a recovery plan in mind. No one is perfect in this process. Knowing what to do when one or both of you go off track is critical. Answers to the question of how we get back on track are part of the Action Plans in the next chapter.

9

Accountability Action Plans

In today's world, a couple cannot afford *not* to be accountable to each other. But there is also value in having other couples in your life who care about you and your marriage and who will be a positive influence. There's little value in being a "loner couple" when faced with the pressures of life.

Both of us grew up in churches that numbered only several hundred people. The congregations were small enough that everyone knew everyone else, and newcomers were recognized as such and welcomed. The older people cared about the young people, and the young people knew and cared about the old folks. They knew each other's names and were interested in each other's lives.

One of Jan's favorite people in her home church was Mrs. Mollisee, an elderly woman who lived alone. While growing up, she and Jan would talk together most every week, keeping tabs on each other even though they were probably sixty years apart in age. Jan knew Mrs. Mollisee was a prayer warrior, and she had a great impact on Jan.

Dave knew an older man, also named David, who took an interest in him, especially during his senior year in high school. Several times after church, the older David took young Dave to lunch and became a positive influence on the choices Dave was making and on the path he was heading down.

Today, in the impersonal age of the large church, that doesn't happen very often. Add to that the fact that the popularity of the extended family has waned, with family members living all over the country. As a result, couples have lost a major source of strength that leaves their marriage and their own nuclear family vulnerable. Instead of the extended family providing strength to a couple, and the connected church family being an accountability factor for couples, we need to create our own accountability connections.

Here are some Action Plans that will help you become more connected and more accountable in ways that will enhance your ability to experience SMART Love.

Action Plan #A1—Make a List

One of the predictors that suggests a couple's marriage will be successful is that the couple has other friends who are couples, and they are friends with each other. It's not that the husband has his married male friends, or that the wife has her married female friends. Those are not predictors of success. Success comes to those couples who have other couples in their lives where both the husband and the wife are friends with the other husband and wife.

Make a list of all the couples you are both connected to in some way. Perhaps you're in a couples' Bible study, or your kids are friends with other kids and you know their parents. There might be some couples you barely know, but you believe you'd enjoy their friendship as a couple. Include them on your list as well.

When your list is complete, refine it. Pull out any and all couples that you feel you are already close to and believe they are trustworthy. They will be on your A-list.

Next, pull out any couples you would like to get to know better. They might be the parents of your kids' friends, or they could just be couples you see at church or school, and when you talk briefly with them, you go away thinking they would be fun to get to know better. They will be on your B-list.

Talk together about your A-list first. Ask yourselves how you can strengthen the connections with one of those couples. How might you get to know this couple better? Perhaps it would be through having them over for dinner or meeting them somewhere for a meal. Be creative and make this a fun project. The next Action Plan will take it a step further.

Action Plan #A2—Start a Couples' Group

Spend some time reflecting on both your A-list and your B-list, pick several couples you think would enjoy each other, and start a group. There are two different possibilities you can explore.

First, consider four or five couples you think would be open to getting together for a weekend. Our group started with one of the wives setting up a ladies' getaway. It took some planning, but it was set for a hotel on the central coast of California, halfway between where we all lived. (It's better not to pick a place too fancy—just a place to relax, talk, and have fun.) While there, the women talked about a lot of things, but one thing they were all interested in was how to include their husbands in the next outing. Boldly, they set a tentative place and date. Each returned home with a sense of excitement about their weekend and a plan for the couples to get together in four months. Dates were confirmed, and three of the five couples (the Northern California group) took on the task of planning the weekend.

During the thirty years we've been meeting, we've been to all kinds of interesting places. We've hiked in the Sierra Nevada mountains, stayed in a condo on the beach, and explored San Diego and San Francisco. We also went to Bodega Bay, where Alfred Hitchcock's movie *The Birds* was filmed. Wherever you live, there are great places to explore. But don't over-plan; always leave time for just being together and talking.

One of the couples who is part of our group started another group of couples, all of whom live in the same area. Now they have two groups. One of our sons just spent a week with two other couples who have been meeting annually for almost ten years. They include their kids on their outings, while our group is just for the couples. There's no set way to do the outing. All it requires is some creative planning that is spread around, and a commitment from each person to always be present.

Second, consider starting a couples' group that meets weekly or biweekly to discuss a book of the Bible or a book like this one. We've found that the best purpose for a group like this is not just to study together but also to include the personal application of what you study. This way the couples get to know each other better and become more accountable to each other.

Remember, the purpose is to develop the kind of connection with other couples that allows you to become loving accountability partners with them. Whichever type of couples' group you start, or whether you start both types, the goal is the kind of friendship that develops trusting relationships in which it is safe to be known by the other couples.

Action Plan #A3—Connect with a Mentor

In addition to developing trusting friends as a couple and being accountable to each other, it is important to have a same-sex mentor in your life. A mentor is an advisor, a guide, and/or a coach who acts as a consultant. They do not fill the role of a parent, although they can be a good parental figure in our lives.

The Bible affirms the value of mentors. Paul taught that older women "should teach others what is good. These older women would train the younger women to love their husbands and their children, to live wisely and be pure, to work in their homes, to do good, and to be submissive to their husbands" (Titus 2:3–4). Obviously, a good female mentor is a woman who exemplifies these characteristics.

Paul goes on to instruct Titus, his mentee, to be a mentor to the young men. He tells him to "encourage the young men to live wisely. And you yourself must be an example to them by doing good works of every kind. Let everything you do reflect the integrity and seriousness of your teaching" (vv. 6–7).

A mentor is not someone who has it all together but one who has integrity and lives in a way that sets a good example. Above all, they need to be trustworthy. If you are young, you need an older person to guide you along the path they have already taken. If you are older, you can still benefit from a mentor. Being older may mean you are already a mentor, but you are also accountable to friends your own age.

My primary accountability partner was a close friend I had since my college days. He died recently, yet he was an example to me of what we often talked about. We were both in some form of ministry, and our goal was to finish well. Many of those in ministry slip and tragically fall—they don't finish well. I can say my friend finished well, and I intend to do the same. Fortunately, I have other close friends who are willing to hold me accountable.

Action Plan #A4—Enhance Sexual Fidelity

Years ago, we heard Charlie and Martha Shedd speak on marriage. During one of their talks, they shared what it was like to live in a beach community that also was a vacation spot. Often, as they would walk the beach, one of them would notice a good-looking man or woman. They would point that person out to their spouse and then give a 1 to 10 rating. They made a fun game out of what they were observing. In this way, everything was out in the open—not much chance of secret thoughts or feelings.

As I reflect on what they shared, I realize it wasn't the rating system, it was more the comfort they had talking with each other about someone else's attractiveness. They modeled an openness that involved being accountable to each other in the area of sexuality.

To get a sense of how comfortable you are talking about sexual issues, take the following quiz out loud together. Read the statement, discuss the possible answers, then pick one. Talk about the statement and your thoughts about why you answered as you did.

1. When I am with my spouse and see an attractive person of the opposite sex:

   A. I look away and say nothing.

   B. I struggle to look away.

   C. I make some kind of honest comment to my spouse.

2. When my spouse expresses a concern about something in my behavior toward someone of the opposite sex:

   A. I tend to defend my innocence.

   B. I change the subject.

   C. I listen and learn.

3. When we see something sexual or sensual on TV or in a movie:

   A. Neither of us says anything.

   B. One of us talks about the decline in morality in our time.

   C. We discuss what we saw and how we really reacted.

4. When I have sexual feelings for my spouse:

   A. I tend to act sexual and hope for the best.

   B. I am quiet and wait for the bedroom.

   C. I can talk openly about my needs and feelings.

5. When I want to try something different in the bedroom:

   A. I can't talk about it, since we don't talk about sex.

   B. I just try.

   C. We can have an open conversation about it.

If you have more "A" answers, you need to talk together more about the issues of attractiveness, lustful feelings, and your own sexual relationship. "A" answers indicate that sex is too much of a closed subject with one or both of you. If you have more "B" answers, you're not much better off, but at least you try. My hope is that you both are comfortable with the "C" answers.

Sex is really one form of communication. If you can't talk about sexual matters with each other, over time it will limit your intimacy together. If it is really difficult for you to talk about sexual things, you may need to work with a counselor to develop more comfort in talking about sex together.

Action Plan #A5—Discuss Money and Power

Who has the power in your marriage? The one who controls the money. Often when a husband who had complete control of the money dies, the wife has no idea how much money she has or even how and where to access the money. This is a tragic circumstance that should never happen! It is the result of a big power play on the part of the husband.

The goal is to see how you can achieve a balance of power in your marriage. That means there is an openness along with a shared responsibility regarding all aspects of money. Here's a list of what both parties may want to be aware of:

Assets:

    Approximate net worth

    Liquid assets (available cash)—where?

    Fixed assets (property)

Liabilities (money owed):

    List of payments and the due dates

Sources of income

At least an approximate budget

Spendable income each month, if any

Talk together about which of these are most important to each of you. Sometimes one person may say, "I don't need to know all this," and that's fine. But regardless of your age, it helps to have a record of all of the above someplace that is available to both of you, and to update it every six months or so. That way, if something happens to the one managing the money, the record is there and is kept where it is always available to the other spouse.

Sometimes one spouse may keep the financial status a secret because it is basically bad news. The net worth is written in red ink. But the point is the same—openness and accountability. If your net worth is in the red, get involved with something like Crown Financial Ministries or Dave Ramsey's program. Either one can provide a doable way out of debt.

Action Plan #A6—Be Spiritually Accountable

We believe that the husband needs to be the initiator for building a spiritually accountable marriage. That may seem old-fashioned, but we've only seen couples develop spiritual intimacy when the husband takes the initiative.

It's like dancing. We've talked with couples who've taken dance lessons, and to the uninitiated, it seems strange that the man is called to lead. The woman is usually the better dancer, probably because she took lessons as a little girl. A man typically doesn't have any experience as a kid with dancing, so he starts as a real beginner. Yet in spite of his lack of practice and his clumsiness, he is the one who's going to lead the couple. It's not hard to imagine what would happen if the woman was told to lead. The man would never learn to dance. He has to bungle his way through the early discomfort and lead his better-equipped-to-dance wife.

The same principle applies to the spiritual side of a couple's marriage. For some reason, women are more comfortable doing spiritual activities with others than the typical male is. Maybe it's because they take part in women's Bible studies, where they learn to be comfortable talking about the Bible, and maybe they are praying out loud around the other women. Unless the husband is a pastor, he probably has very little experience doing spiritual activities with other people. And even then, a male pastor doing spiritual activities together with just his wife feels an awkwardness like that of the first dance lesson. The same is true for men in general.

A good way to begin is by having the husband take the initiative to reserve seven minutes a day, four times a week, to read a passage of the Bible together. Or let him initiate a time when you both pray together, just the two of you. If one of you is not comfortable praying out loud, then try this: First, talk about the things you want to pray about. Then take each other's hands while the husband says, "Let's pray." You each pray silently, and when you are finished, you squeeze your spouse's hands, and when they are finished, they squeeze your hands. You've just prayed together!

It's the intentionality that is important. You have just intentionally prayed together. Gradually, over time, one of you may say "amen" out loud, and then at some point you may actually pray out loud together. That's the goal. One woman said that when she heard her husband pray for their kids, she could actually hear his heart for them.

The goal over time is to become comfortable doing spiritual things together, including taking each other's spiritual temperature, so to speak. Can you and your spouse sit together and talk about how each of you is doing spiritually? That's the ultimate goal of being accountable spiritually.

Remember, not only are the spiritual activities initiated by the husband, but making spiritual activities a consistent and ongoing part of the marriage is also his responsibility.

Action Plan #A7—Parent from the Same Page

One of the devious behaviors any young kid will develop is becoming a wedge between Mom and Dad. If young Sammy asks Mom to do something and she says no, and then a little later he asks Dad if he can do the same thing and Dad says yes, you can easily see the potential for conflict between the parents. And that marriage is headed for trouble.

Imagine the scene: Sammy does what he wanted to do. Mom gets mad and prepares to discipline him. But before she can, Sammy says to her, "Dad told me I could!" Now the issue isn't between Mom and Sammy but between Mom and Dad. And Sammy gets to skate on the problem, at least for a while.

That's a simple situation in which it is clear how the problem started. It wasn't based on different philosophies of parenting.

As our starting point for how we parent, we all face either the repetition of what we experienced growing up or a complete reaction against it. Typically, couples are drawn together without knowing whether or not they agree on how to parent. They may have talked about it, but until the children arrive, the conversation is often very idealistic.

Begin your discussion by defining as best you can your basic parenting style. Are you more permissive than your spouse? Are you more of an authoritarian as a parent? Or are you more of a laissez-faire parent who is hands-off until a crisis hits home? Where do you agree about parenting issues, and where do you disagree? To help you remember, think about your last argument over a parenting issue.

In the previous chapter, we talked about the balance between being kind and being firm in our parenting. Which direction do you tend to go when kindness and firmness get out of balance? When you go one way, it's almost a guarantee that your spouse will go the opposite. It's just human nature to do so. That is, unless you are aware of your own contribution to the problem. If you have trouble getting on the same page with each other, get a book on parenting and read it together. Whether or not you agree with the premise of the book, it will give you a common starting point for discussing how to compromise and reach a common approach in your parenting behavior.

If that doesn't work, talk with one of your couple friends who seem to be calm and collected in their parenting. Ask them what they do as parents, and what they would do in your situation. Part of why you are developing these trusted friendships is to be accountable to each other as couples. This may be the time and the situation for that.

Action Plan #A8—Manage Your Schedules

One of the things we would do at our Friday morning breakfast ritual was synchronize our schedules. Each week we would talk about what was on the schedule for the next week. Then every couple of weeks, we would take out our calendars and compare them to see that we both knew what was going on schedule-wise. Other couples we know have a master calendar that they keep in plain view in their kitchen. Whenever something needs to be put on the calendar, they not only write it down, but they also tell their spouse what they wrote and what the event is about.

But what do you do when the schedule is out of control? That's when you have to learn to say no to some things. Sometimes the things you are asked to do sound so inviting that you want to say an instant yes. But remember, you're a couple, and what one person does affects the other. Make a habit of saying, "Let me check with my spouse, and I'll get back to you."

The problem with many of our schedules today is that they are compounded by our kids' schedules. It's kind of an in thing to be child centered. For many couples, their lives are run by their kids' schedules. So sometimes the "no" isn't about something the parents are asked to do; it's something we are expected to do for our kids.

This doesn't mean you cut back on what you're doing with your kids. It does mean that you become more serious about the choices you and your kids are making. It is okay to say no to something one of your kids wants to do because you're exhausted. If they can make it happen another way, fine. But you have the choice to say no.

It all boils down to you as a couple focusing more on the choices you have, where you say yes or no. But it also involves teaching each other, as well as others in your family, how to make good choices.

It always helps to have some family rituals in place that cannot be violated by any individual. If Sunday night is family night, with a special menu, various activities, and time spent with the family, it's much easier to be able to say no than if there are no rituals in place. So not only do you work with the calendar, but you also focus on creating some meaningful rituals that can be enjoyed by all of you and benefit the sense of family.

Action Plan #A9—Examine Your Honesty Quotient

Since we said that everyone lies at times, let's begin by remembering some of the white lies we've told, or the lies of omission we are guilty of committing. But let's keep the examples out of the marriage relationship. Think of a time when you lied in one way or another in a relationship other than your marriage. Share the story with your spouse.

Often we stretch the truth with our kids or with other family members. We don't have the energy to do something with someone when they ask, so we tell them a white lie: "I already have a commitment for that evening." Our rationale is that "everyone does it." And everyone does do it. But it works against our trustworthiness.

Our first lie as a young person was usually designed to avoid some kind of punishment. In some ways, we still lie in order to avoid punishment, or at least the punishing hassle we would create if we were truthful. But couples in great marriages have learned how to be truthful with each other. The underlying principle is found in Ephesians 4:15, where Paul says we are to "speak the truth in love." A little later on in the chapter he adds, "Let us tell our neighbors [including our spouse] the truth, for we are all parts of the same body" (v. 25). What Paul is saying is a reflection of what the Old Testament prophet Zechariah said: "But this is what you must do: Tell the truth to each other" (8:16).

The problem is that if we are to "speak the truth in love," it is a two-way street. It also involves *hearing* the truth in love. When a wife responds to her husband's question about his weight, she needs to be truthful and loving as she says, "Yes, your weight bothers me." But he also needs to be loving in his acceptance of her truthful statement and not become defensive or resentful.

How do we tell each other the truth in love? For starters, we need to soften the way we begin. I was working with a couple, and Amy discussed how Joe had confronted her about something I had asked them to do in the previous session. Amy was hurt and angry.

I asked Joe, "Can you soften how you begin your question and ask her again?"

He tried, but Amy was still angry and said to him, "See, you're still blaming me, and I'm tired of it."

"What were you trying to find out from Amy?" I asked him.

"I really just wanted to know how she felt about the assignment. I didn't think I was blaming her for anything."

135

"Why don't you soften even more what you say and be more specific in what you are asking?" I suggested.

So he said to Amy, "I'm not blaming you, I'm just interested in how you felt about the assignment."

This time Amy was able to respond. It takes practice to soften what we say to each other, but that's the "in love" part of what Paul tells us.

In order to hear what the other person is saying in love, we need to remind ourselves to accept each other's imperfections. Neither of us is perfect, nor are we going to say things perfectly. Take a minute and talk about a recent misunderstanding that you had with each other in which one or both of you misread your spouse's statement or motivation.

The other problem we encounter is our tendency to personalize what our spouse says to us. Sometimes the speaker can defuse this tendency by beginning with something like, "I know we tend to personalize difficult conversations, and I don't want you to think I'm attacking you. I just need for you to hear what I'm saying." Remember, while the goal is to speak the truth in love, we have to work even harder at hearing the truth in love as well.

Action Plan #A10—Decide What You Will Do When You Get Off Track

Growth is an uneven process. We take two steps forward and feel like we've got it, and then we fall back into an old pattern. I worked with a couple who came up with a plan for what to do when one of them felt hurt by something the other said or did. They were to simply say something like,

"That hurt me," and the other person could not explain or defend their behavior. They would just apologize.

They were really good at following through with their plan, using hand signals whenever one would be tempted to explain or defend their behavior. They had agreed they would not do that.

After they had been successful for several weeks, I asked what they would do if one of them broke the rule and started to defend themselves, and the other got caught up in a counter defense—in other words, what they would do when the old pattern suddenly reemerged. They didn't know, for both of them hadn't yet gotten off track.

We talked and came up with a plan for getting back on track. They decided one of them would use a time-out signal that would be honored by the other person. Then they were to say something like, "We're back to the old pattern. Let's start over." And of course, they soon had an opportunity to implement their plan to get back on track.

What's your plan for how to reboot when one or both of you gets off track? Being prepared for the inevitable usually works, if it's been agreed upon in a nonthreatening time in the relationship. Don't become obsessive about doing the right things all the time, and don't set up an expectation that everything is good and the old patterns are behind you. Paul reminds us, "If you think you are standing strong, be careful not to fall" (1 Cor. 10:12). Go slow, but stay the course!

10

R—Reading the Other Person's Emotions

As you have worked your way through the first three sets of Action Plans, you've begun building a good foundation for the last two competencies of SMART Love. You are growing in your self-awareness of your emotions and in being able to manage your emotions. These are individual skills that you are developing. We've added the interactive competency of becoming more accountable to each other. And now for the last two interactive competencies.

To develop these last two skill sets requires that you work together as a couple. You will find that these skills build on how successful you have been with applying the earlier skill sets. Our being able to read our spouse's emotions requires that we be aware of our own emotions, and it will lead to our becoming more comfortable as we work together as a team in understanding each other's emotions.

Empathy

Reading the other person's emotions basically describes our ability to be empathic. Empathy is something we have all experienced at some time or another. We can easily recognize it when we receive it from someone. We've all had teachers who we felt really understood us. They sensed we were struggling with something, and when they talked to us, we just knew they understood. Or we might have had the same feeling with a friend who really got what we were experiencing emotionally. We might not have used the word *empathy*, but that's what it was.

The word *empathy* was brought into the English language from the Greek word *empatheia*, which literally means "feeling into." It describes the ability for someone to perceive, and in some ways feel, the subjective experience of another person. Empathy involves the ability and the willingness to understand another person's thoughts, feelings, and struggles from their perspective. It allows the other person to express their emotions while we respect their boundaries. It involves listening to more than just the words. Empathy does not mean solving the problem, agreeing, analyzing, or arguing, as these may close down the other person's emotions.

Taking the other person's perspective in a situation requires that we know our own emotional worlds and are able to separate our emotions and expectations from theirs. It requires the ability to be sincerely interested in what the other person is experiencing in silence or with words. It is a shared process of listening and responding while we suspend our own personal biases to make room in our thoughts and emotions so that we can share in their personal world. Empathy often transforms the listener simply by the experience of entering into the other person's world.

The other person senses our empathy as we listen and notice their facial expressions, their body language in general, their posture, the tone of their voice, and other deeper intuitive things that are expressed nonverbally. That's why understanding nonverbal parts of communication is so vital to empathizing. When one's nonverbal communication contradicts their verbal communication, we will always believe the nonverbal. It's deeper than the obvious and more accurate. More than 90 percent of the messages we give each other, in our marriage and elsewhere, are nonverbal. That's because the heart usually sees things rightly, for it pays attention to our own intuition and to the nonverbal.

Empathy is different from sympathy. When you express sympathy for someone, you are saying you have compassion for that person, but you don't feel what they do. Sympathy can also have broader applications. For example, we may have sympathy with a cause or with a group of people. We may watch our favorite team lose the final playoff and feel sadness for them. Sympathy is the ability to feel and express caring and understanding. It may lead us to want to help a group or person in need, but it is simply caring and not an emotional identification. Empathy is always a shared emotional experience with another person.

When we are able to be empathic, especially with our spouse, the benefits are immeasurable. They include being more sensitive and better adjusted emotionally in our own lives. In the context of SMART Love, learning how to show empathy leads us to experience a richer and more fulfilling marriage.

The Roots of Empathy

The foundation of our ability to be empathic as adults is laid early in our lives. For example, if you've been around a group of toddlers, you may have had the experience of watching one of them fall down and start to cry. Pretty soon others are crying, and if your child is there, eventually they start crying and come to you for comfort, even though they didn't fall down and hurt themselves. The roots of empathy begin to develop from the day we are born. In a nursery filled with newborn babies, when one of them cries, the others react with tears as if the problem one child is having is their own.

This is explained by the fact that we are delivered into this life with "mirror neurons" in our brains. These are designed to very quickly help us learn how to do things by watching and mirroring others. Because the mind is so primitive at this early age, it mirrors all kinds of things, including the hurt another child experiences. Through mirroring, the child interprets what another child is experiencing as if it were their own. These mirror neurons are the foundation, it is believed, for our developing the ability to be empathic.

By the time we are eighteen months to two years old, instead of mirroring the crying child, we will now reach out and try to comfort them, without understanding what we are doing. We may retrieve the child's security blanket, take them one of our toys, or even seek the aid of a parent to comfort them. Some even suggest that, at this early age, the better way to discipline your child who did something wrong is to point out how their behavior affected someone else, not to tell them that what they did was wrong or bad.

By the age of four, our brains are more structured, and now we begin to understand what we're doing. And by the time we enter elementary school, we are able to naturally feel empathy for other kids in pain.

Again, the amygdala is involved. There are a large number of connections between the amygdala and the prefrontal cortex that are constantly reading another person's face and voice for evidence of what they are feeling. They are also constantly reading what we are doing as we speak and listen.

For example, if I were talking with you, my amygdala would relay information to my prefrontal cortex, which is the decision-making part of my brain. It might say things like, "Careful, he's getting upset," which causes my prefrontal cortex to adjust how I am saying something to you. Then it tells me, "That's better, he's calming down. Careful how you say it." Of course, that's illustrative, not actual. The amygdala doesn't talk, but in a microsecond it is communicating this type of information to the executive part of my brain.

Your amygdala is doing the same dance as it evaluates what I am saying to you. It's reading my five senses and using your five senses, along with our intuitions, to instruct your executive brain how to adjust what you're doing and saying. It's like a symphony of the amygdalae, and the idea is to get them to effectively tune in to each other to create the possibility of empathy and attunement.

Attunement

What we are describing in the dance of our amygdalae is how we tune in to each other as couples to let the other person know we understand. Attunement is being in or bringing into harmony—a feeling of being "at one" with another person.

We once watched a video that highlighted the importance of attunement by showing a mother and her infant, who was probably about nine months old. It was a designed experiment in which, for a certain period of time, the mother was to look into her infant child's eyes and interact with him. The infant was animated, laughing, and totally responding to his mother. They were in harmony with each other.

Then the mother was told to break eye contact and look away from the infant. It didn't take long for the little guy to start to make noise, to fuss and wave his arms—all trying to get his mother's attention again. Finally, the child started to cry, and the mother was told to reengage with her son. Gradually, the infant calmed down and reengaged with his mother. That was an example of attunement, misattunement, and reattunement.

When we're infants, emotional attunement is the basis for our building a strong, secure attachment with both mother and father. The attachment formed in infancy is typically consistent with our later adult attachments, and especially the attachment we form with our spouse. If you did not have the benefit of forming a secure attachment with a loving parent in infancy, your marriage relationship may be challenging. But when you as a couple are attuned to each other's emotions, it can be part of the healing of the insecure attachment styles you may have brought to the marriage from childhood.

Secure adult attachments provide the safety needed to experience empathy with each other in marriage. They also correlate with better health, lower depression, and less anxiety. Secure attachments make us better lovers and better parents. When we can look at our spouse with attention and tune in to what they are feeling and experiencing, it is calming, and it fosters a deep connection. It's the same thing the infant experienced when his mother really tuned in to what he needed.

So what happens when we get out of tune with each other? The same thing that happened to the infant. We experience immediate distress, and if the misattunement goes on for any length of time, a growing passivity and negativity about the relationship develops. Over time, both the child and the adult will shut down their emotions, even obliterating them from their awareness. Or the child will selectively discover that certain emotions are okay to express, but they must shut off those deemed not okay. Fortunately, what gets shut off can also be rediscovered and reintegrated in a nurturing marital relationship.

Trust and Attunement

At the root of our being able to develop empathy with each other and being in tune with each other is the important issue of trust. When in a relationship, we ask questions like, "Can I trust you to be there and listen to me when I'm upset? Will you prejudge me? Can I trust you to make me your priority over other family, friends, and even your work? Can I trust you to respect me?" On PsycINFO, the research database used by psychologists, there are over one hundred thousand references to the word *trust*. Trust is a big issue in life, especially in marriage.

Trust is essential in all areas of life. It's important to be able to trust a neighbor or a merchant. In fact, trustworthiness is one of the most important qualities in deciding who to date and then who to marry. When we think of betrayal, the destroyer of trust, we typically think of big things like infidelity, but research says that betrayal can be very small and can happen in just one instance. The act may seem like a small thing, but if it touched a raw nerve in the one betrayed, it's betrayal.

Just as betrayal may be felt over something that appears small, building and rebuilding trust is based on many small moments and equally small behaviors over time. Researcher John Gottman says that behaviors that "turn towards" the other person help build trust, while behaviors that "turn away" from the other person can be felt as small betrayals and eat away at our ability to trust. A key example of how we "turn towards" is when we face up to a difficult situation and choose to interact regarding the issue. We "turn away" when we choose to ignore the situation and act like it didn't happen, or we avoid talking about it.

The more we "turn towards" our spouse, the more we build trust, and the more we build trust, the more attuned we are to each other. And the more attuned we are to each other, the easier it is to respond to our spouse with empathy. But it takes time, as Don and Pat now realize. They had to face their trust issues with each other. It took time for them to respond to the changes they were each making in their communication. For what seemed like too long, they responded as if the other person were acting in the old ways, and they would brace themselves for the anger. But gradually, they became comfortable with the new patterns of trusting and becoming more attuned to each other.

Types of Empathy

When your spouse sincerely says to you, "I feel your frustration," it may sound like empathy, but is it really? If so, what type of empathy is it? There are basically three ways to interpret that statement. The first is *cognitive empathy*, which indicates your spouse at least understands your perspective. They are able to see the situation from your point of view. They understand, at least intellectually. But cognitive empathy is really more a form of being sympathetic. It falls short of being empathic, at least in the way we have defined empathy.

The second type is *empathic concern*, where your spouse recognizes what you are feeling—they are attuned to your emotion—and show a genuine concern. But again, this isn't true empathy. There is no shared emotional experience, where they enter into your frustration. This could be called "being compassionate," but it still falls short of how we have defined empathy.

The third type is *personalized empathy*, where your spouse actually feels your pain, distress, and emotion. This fits our definition of empathy. You can get a feel for personalized empathy when you watch a suspenseful movie. As the action increases and the tension mounts, you notice you are feeling more tense, and when the feared object suddenly appears on the screen, you may jump in your seat and even shout something like, "Watch out!" The actors have successfully personalized their situation, and you have genuinely experienced true empathy.

Obstacles to Developing the Skill of Empathy

We've seen that the foundation for our adult capacity for empathy was set in motion when we were very young. None of us experienced perfection along the way, and our deficits in our ability to be empathic are based on failures in how attuned our parents were with our emotions when we were toddlers and children.

Our first obstacle in our struggle with this competency of SMART Love is falling short in our ability to express empathy. That means we will have a tendency to set off negative reactions in our spouse and in our family. We will not be sensitive to the moods of the important people in our lives and will create problems rather than resolve them.

Even when the deficits are minor, we may still resist being empathic with our spouse. Empathy only goes in one direction at a time. So one of us has to go first, and we may not like that idea, because it means we are to meet the needs of the other before we get our needs met. Empathy takes us from being selfish to being sacrificial.

The second obstacle is a more common problem. I worked with a couple where the husband could not break free of the idea that empathy meant he had to agree with his wife's perspective. As a result, he was seldom supportive of his wife, since he believed that being supportive meant agreement. Empathy has nothing to do with agreeing or determining who is right and who is wrong. It is simply experiencing the emotional responses of our spouse and allowing ourselves to be attuned to their perspective.

The third common obstacle is the fear that we will get it wrong. One of the things I do as a counselor is try to enter the emotional world of the person sitting across from me. I remember early in my practice having this fear: what if I get it wrong and totally miss the other person's perspective? I had to face that fear, and I found it to be groundless. Over the years, I have usually gotten pretty close to being right. But when I do miss it, the other person is gracious and corrects me. I think that making the effort to be more empathic will feel so good, your spouse will willingly correct what you may have missed.

Finally, as we said in one of our earlier Action Plans, we have to be willing to be emotionally uncomfortable. Being empathic will take us into some painful emotions, both in what we experience with our spouse and in what gets stirred up within ourselves. Discomfort is going to be part of our being empathic, but the rewards more than make up for the pain of the moment.

Becoming more empathic boils down to developing our ability to be a good listener. As a culture, we are not very good at listening. It's a lost art. We have what I like to call "the *People* magazine attention span." If something is going to take more than two pages or more than two or three minutes, we lose interest and want to go on to some other subject. But empathy, attunement, and trust all take time.

I sometimes joke with an audience by telling the men that good listening is simply learning when and how often to say "uh-huh." After all, that's what the stereotypes portray a counselor as doing. At least it indicates that we are still listening. There is an art to listening that requires us to focus our attention on the speaker, and every now and then we restate something they just said so they know we really are listening. Jesus said in Matthew 11:15, "Anyone with ears to hear should listen and understand!" He couples hearing with understanding.

I've also found that for men, it's hard to resist the urge to fix what their wife is dealing with. Men's brains are designed to listen, get the picture, and then offer a solution. Men love to fix things. Women's brains are designed to want to talk. There are exceptions, but these characteristics of how men listen and how women talk are generally true. So both have to work harder at listening.

Jerry struggled with this. Once he came out of his silent routine and started to interact with Kimberly, he wanted to solve all of her problems. He had to learn that she just wanted him to listen and respond. At first he said it didn't feel like a manly thing to do—just listen. But when he experienced Kimberly slowing down now that she felt listened to, it got easier over time.

The interesting thing that happens when the man does listen is that what he thought he needed to fix already got fixed by his willingness to listen. Add in attunement, and you're well on your way to enriching your ability to be empathic.

Empathy Action Plans

We move now from Action Plans that look inward to those that look outward toward our interaction with others, in particular with our spouse. We want to learn more about our spouse and grow in our appreciation of them. To improve our ability to do so, we will look at our capacity to experience empathy in several different situations. For example, you and your spouse may go sit in a mall and watch people's body language as they walk by, thereby becoming more aware of the need and the ability to read the emotions of your spouse. Or you may work on becoming a better listener by focusing in as a co-worker complains to you about some job situation, or as your spouse explains something they are concerned about.

As you work on developing the ability to be empathic, you will continue to work on being more aware of your own emotions and improve how you are managing your emotions. Hopefully, you will also be enjoying the other couples you are spending more time with. These are the foundation blocks for being more empathic with those you care for most. Being comfortable with your own emotions sets the stage for being able to experience someone else's emotions.

You can have a lot of fun with the ten Action Plans that follow. You will find that some of them will be on your mind as you shop, work, or even stand in line at the grocery store. You are going to become a skilled people watcher. Enjoy it as you grow!

Action Plan #R1—Spend Time People Watching

Take some time to people watch. Find someplace comfortable and watch the world go by. While sitting in a mall or a coffee shop, notice things like what people do with their eyes. Do they look at you, or do they avoid looking at you? What does their face reveal about their mood or their emotion? How fast are they walking? This is the introduction to the next Action Plan, which looks more specifically at body language. In this Action Plan, all you are doing is getting comfortable watching other people.

As you and your spouse do this together, talk about what you observe. When you go out to eat, watch the other people and talk about what you see. The goal is to become more observant of other people as a fun introduction into more advanced people watching.

Action Plan #R2—Pay Attention to Body Language

We talked earlier about how our faces speak the universal language of the emotions. So begin with showing each other what the basic emotions look like on your faces. Show your spouse an angry face, a fearful face, a sad face, and a shameful face. Include the positive emotions and show each other a joyful face and a surprised face.

In understanding body language, you always begin with the face. Look at the eyebrows. Are they raised or lowered? What about the mouth? Is it relaxed, or does it look tense? Look especially at the eyes. Are they looking away? Are they shifting? Is there too much blinking? Can the person look you in the eye? Are they relaxed? Then look at the head. Is it tilted? Where is the person looking? Are they saying yes but shaking their head no? Are they looking down? All of these are the primary "words" of body language.

To better hone our skills, it helps to compare notes. Reading body language is a complex art, and you both are probably beginners in how to interpret the different expressions. You also need to listen to your intuition, for it is usually in tune with body language.

We also have what are called "micro expressions." When someone wants to hide an emotion, they will try to prevent it from showing on their face and body. But they can't hide it completely, so there will be a micro expression that gives it away. Let's say someone is angry but doesn't want anyone to know it. In a microsecond before they give a fake smile, the expression of anger will show on their face, and then it will disappear. It takes practice to pick up micro expressions, but they can be caught if you're watching for them.

Once you are somewhat comfortable reading the face and the head, move to the shoulders, the torso, and the arms and legs. Are the shoulders back? That can indicate either confidence or hostility, depending on other signs. Notice if the arms are crossed. Has the other person turned their body partially away from you, or are they facing you? Are any arm gestures close to the body and tight? Does the person act distracted, such as noticing you have some lint on your shoulder and reaching to pick it off? Notice especially the gestures that seem spontaneous and exaggerated.

The body language shown when someone is lying is something everyone is curious about. Ex-CIA specialists on TV tell how they detect a person is lying, especially with micro expressions. One of the things they notice is where a person's hand is while they talk. A possible indicator of someone lying is speaking with their hand or fingers in front of their mouth, as if they are trying to hide what they are saying. When a person is lying, their eyes move rapidly, and they don't maintain eye contact. Their breathing increases, and their voice changes. Be careful, though—these are generalizations and can also indicate that the other person is simply nervous.

As you people watch, develop your skills to work at reading body language in general. For example, I was once watching a family walking in a line at a restaurant, one behind the other. The teenage daughter was at the end of the line, and her body language had "I don't want to be here!" written all over it. Her head was down, she looked both angry and sad, and her shoulders were slumped forward as if she had been forced to come on this outing with her family. She obviously did not want to be there.

Now, I could be very wrong. If Jan had been with me, I would have pointed out the family and listened to determine if she saw the same things I did. She might not have. To her, the young woman may have appeared to be feeling sick, or she may have just been disciplined by one of her parents, or she may have just gotten the short end of some deal with her younger brother.

No one is an expert, but we are all learning. And as we learn to watch other people, we develop our sensitivity and ability to read our spouse's nonverbal messages as well.

Action Plan #R3—Work on the Three A's of Empathy

On the way to building our skill of empathy, we may feel we are so out of touch with each other that developing empathy seems impossible. Many people struggle with just getting their spouse's attention. Here are three A's that will help you get back in touch with each other.

The first A is to simply carve out some time when you can each *attend* to the other person. Take advantage of any time that you are both together without distractions as an opportunity to just be together and to connect with each other. I've suggested to couples that they take fifteen minutes after dinner to just sit and talk as friends. No problem solving! The foundation of a healthy marriage is the marital friendship. When you can, just sit and talk about all the mundane things that happened during your day, just like you might do with a friend.

If your date night involves going to a movie, there's usually not much connecting happening while you watch it. It's too much like sitting at home and watching TV. You're sitting side by side, not facing each other. Therefore, your focus is not on each other but on the screen. Nothing wrong with that; it's just not a connecting behavior. If you go to a movie on your date night, plan to go out afterward and talk about what you just watched. Or if you're watching something on

TV, turn off the TV when the show ends and talk about what you just watched. Attending to each other doesn't involve deep, heavy conversations. Begin by keeping it light so you can strengthen your friendship.

The second A to work on is your *attachment* to each other. There are three behaviors that, taken together, form an attached, bonded connection with another person. First, the other person needs to be available. Only when there is availability is there the potential for attachment. Think about this in terms of a child. How can there be an attachment if the mother and father are not available to the child? There can't be, and when we are too busy with life and family and are unavailable to our spouse, the attachment suffers.

Another part of attachment is responsiveness. We may be available to our spouse, but if we are unresponsive to them, the attachment will suffer. Mom may have been available when we were a kid, but if she was so preoccupied with her own world that she wasn't responsive to us when we needed her attention, the attachment was weak and insecure.

The last piece that builds an attachment is to experience acceptance. If I feel you accept me and are both available and responsive, there will be a secure attachment.

The third A of getting back in touch is that we are able to experience *attunement* with each other. This means we are tuned in to our spouse even, and especially, when we aren't together. It's hard to be attuned to someone when they are "out of sight, out of mind." But when we are attending to our spouse, securely attached to them, and in tune with them, we will develop an awareness of them, just as we do with our kids. We carry their concerns with us at all times. That's laying a foundation for building empathy.

Action Plan #R4—Overcome Barriers to Empathy

In the previous chapter, we highlighted four obstacles that can limit our ability to be empathic, which are summarized below. Take some time together to talk about each one.

1. Someone has to take the initiative and start the empathy cycle. How do you understand empathy to be a one-way street? Is there anything that makes it hard for either of you to "go first"?

2. Thinking that somehow one spouse is agreeing with the other if they are empathic can be a major stumbling block. How do you handle the possible conflict between being empathic and agreeing with the other person? How can you be empathic when you don't agree with why the other person is feeling what they are feeling?

3. To be empathic can be a messy process. We don't always get it right at first. Think of examples when you have experienced some degree of empathy from someone and had to help them more clearly understand what you were experiencing. Why do we sometimes think we have to get it right if we're going to be empathic?

4. Sometimes our instant reaction to showing empathy is that we don't want to enter into the feelings of our spouse. They are too painful, and we realize we may be responsible for those feelings. How do we separate what we are feeling from what the other person is feeling? How do we learn to lean in to our own painful emotions so we can enter into our spouse's? How can we help each other do that?

Action Plan #R5—Develop Basic Empathy Skills

Let's assume you both are able to be empathic at least at some level with each other but wish you could deepen your skills. Where do you begin that process? For starters, to remember when you first met each other. Then think back to the time after you had started dating and realized, "This is the one." Talk together as you answer the following questions:

1. What first attracted you to each other?
2. What did you enjoy doing together?
3. Which of the following did you experience during that falling-in-love time?

   Needed less sleep and ate less

   Made that person your priority

   Thought about that person often when apart

   Looked forward to being together

   Laughed a lot and were playful

   Talked together endlessly

   Accepted each other's differences

Don't get upset if you don't experience all of these right now—they are the symptoms of couples falling in love. They make up what has been called an "altered state of consciousness," and fortunately, they don't last for more than a couple of years. They may come and go at times and appear at varying degrees, but they can't be maintained. Yet recapturing the memory of those days gives you a great setting to describe three things you can do today.

First, help your spouse understand they have a place in your heart. Stop talking to yourself about what's missing in your marriage relationship, and rediscover why you chose them to be your spouse. Practice daily the sense of awe at the uniqueness of your spouse as you remember some of those early feelings of interest, love, and acceptance.

Next, open yourself to what your spouse is experiencing emotionally—good or painful. We did that automatically in the early days before we tied the knot. Perhaps you've become too task oriented, too insecure on the job front, or too overwhelmed by the family and the kids to pay attention to what your spouse is feeling. Take the time to find out what in the present makes your spouse happy or sad or scared. Rediscover things like their favorite movie, favorite food, or favorite activity. Be willing to work at loving your spouse unconditionally—like you did at the beginning.

Finally, when you find out what your spouse is feeling, validate those feelings. Don't problem solve—as we said earlier, just listen. One husband told his wife he wanted to hear about as many of her painful feelings as she was willing to share with him. He promised that he would simply listen. He wouldn't jump in to explain or defend himself; the focus would be solely on her and what she described as her feelings.

She didn't think he could do that but took him at his word. She made several pages of notes, and they sat down for him to listen. She launched in and went through her list and then some. He surprised her as he not only listened carefully but also took notes. It led to many other sessions with both of them talking because he simply listened. He communicated to her by his behavior that he valued what she had to share.

Action Plan #R6—Practice Listening

Listening is hard work. We not only have to focus on what is being said, but we also have to be aware in some way of what is not being said. I've worked with wives who think their husband is not listening, and the wife finally says, "You're not listening!" So he repeats to her word-for-word what she just said. That stops her for a moment, and then she typically says something like, "That may be what I said, but you didn't really hear me."

He's confused until I suggest that maybe what she meant was that he didn't really hear her heart. He heard the words, but he didn't hear the passion, the concern, or even the emotion behind what she was saying. Listening isn't just about hearing the words—it doesn't take much effort to parrot those. When we are skilled listeners, we have learned how to pay attention to the nonverbal information—to hear not only the words but also what lies just below the surface.

Here are some suggestions on how to really listen. When your spouse wants to talk, stop everything else and sit down close. Then look her in the eyes as she talks. I've suggested to some men that they put their hand on their wife's forearm. It helps her feel connected as he listens and helps him to focus on what is being said. Don't listen so long that you lose track of what the other person is saying; ask them to pause a minute and let you try to summarize in your own words what you've just heard. Then ask them to continue.

I've suggested couples do the following when the topic is potentially volatile. They are to do this at a specific time once a day until the issue is either resolved or clarified. Each person is to have a pad of paper and a pen, for it is important to take notes. Either one can begin, and they have fifteen minutes, with no interruptions, to make their case. After that time, the other person gets fifteen minutes to make their case without interruptions. The catch is, you cannot respond in this session to anything your spouse has said. That's why you both have to take notes. In tomorrow's session, each person's fifteen minutes are used to add anything new and to respond to what the spouse said yesterday. The other rule is that the subject can only be discussed in the formal thirty-minute time frame. No talking about the subject at other times!

There is always a twenty-four-hour delay in responding to, correcting, or countering something said by the spouse. The delay forces you to take notes, which communicates that you are serious about listening. I've asked couples to do this who used to spend hours arguing about a specific subject. At the end of a week or two of following these guidelines, they came in and told me they finally ran out of things to say. They couldn't fill even five minutes, let alone the fifteen-minute allotment. If you're stuck on some subject and can't get a handle on it, try this exercise.

Action Plan #R7—Live More in the Now

Living more in the present means we have resolved the issues of the past and are more trusting about the future, which leaves us more open to the here and now. The basic emotions that can become oriented to the past are anger and shame, which usually lead into depression. We get stuck living in the past if we consistently ruminate about what we should or shouldn't have done, or what someone else should or shouldn't have done. We struggle with the guilt of toxic shame and keep trying to remake the past so we don't feel so angry, guilty, or shameful.

When we are caught up in the past, we are at some level trying to remake the past into something more acceptable. That may work for a moment, but soon we're back trying again to fix what we thought we had remade. The obvious point is the past cannot ever be remade. It is what it is. So how do we resolve the past? The same way God has resolved it—through forgiveness.

In *The Prince of Tides*, Tom Wingo, the main character, says, "In families there are no crimes beyond forgiveness."[1] That is a biblically sound principle. God's plan is for us to release the past so we can enjoy the present, and to do that we are called to forgive. We need to forgive others who have wronged us, and probably the hardest part of it all is that we need to forgive ourselves as well.

As believers, we can say, as Tom Wingo did, that there is nothing beyond our ability to forgive. Why? Because of how much we have been forgiven. God took the debt of our sin, which we could never repay, and canceled it through the cross when he gave his Son to die in our place (see Col. 2:13–14). He forgave us when we didn't deserve it, so that's how we can resolve the issues of the past—we forgive!

The basic emotion of the future is fear, and with it often come anxiety and worry. If we continually live in the future, ruminating on our fears and worries, we effectively shut down our experience of the present. In Matthew 6, Jesus gives us the reason that worry, along with fear and anxiety, is not to be part of our daily living. In verse 24 he says, "No one can serve two masters. For you will hate one and love the other, you will be devoted to one and despise the other. You cannot serve God and be enslaved to money."

Now, he's not just talking about money, although that is probably one of the main things we worry about. He's asking, "Whom are you going to trust—are you going to trust God, or are you going to try to control the future with whatever you fear and worry about?" That question is clear from the verses that follow: "That is why I tell you not to worry about everyday life.... Can all your worries add a single moment to your life? And why worry about your clothing? ... Why do you have so little faith? So don't worry about these things" (vv. 25, 27–28, 30–31).

When I fear the future and am anxious or worried, I am choosing to trust in my fear, worry, and anxiety. It's like I'm saying to God, "I'll take care of these things with my worry. I'll try to trust you with everything else." So the principle is at the end of verse 24, where Jesus says you cannot serve both God *and* whatever you fear or worry about. Fear, worry, and anxiety all bring into focus what or whom we are going to trust.

As you clear up the issues of the past and of the future, you are released to fully live in the present. Make it a habit to enjoy the present moment. You can still make plans for the future, but not at the expense of the present. You can still remember the past, but not at the expense of the present. Be fully present with your spouse and with your family and friends.

If we are going to respond with empathy, we have to be living in the present.[2]

Action Plan #R8—Avoid the Lies We So Easily Believe

Whether we lie to ourselves or someone else lies to us, there are three lies we tend to fall back into that will short-circuit our ability to be empathic. Take some time to evaluate whether or not you've used any of them with each other.

1. "Your pain and suffering isn't that serious." A variant of this lie is "Your pain and suffering isn't as bad as mine." We are tempted to respond this way when we are caught up in the quest for "fairness," or when it feels like we are in competition over who hurts the most. The basic problem with this lie is that it has shifted the focus from the other person onto myself, and empathy is always about the other person. Another problem is that someone has to go first to be empathic, and this statement is a way to avoid that. So defeat the lie and go first.

2. "You helped create this problem. It's partly your fault." Now we are getting sidetracked into who's to blame. The blame game never takes us anyplace constructive. Blame is like a downward spiral, where you say it is my fault, and then I say in return, "But I only did or said that because you did or said . . ." Then we keep going backward in time in our attempt to place blame. And so on it goes, until we get back to Adam in the Garden of Eden. God asked him why he did what he did, and he said, "It was because of that woman. She made me do it, and by the way, you're the one who put her here with me." God looked at Eve, and she glanced around for someone to blame, but there was no one else. Then

she remembered, "It was that serpent—he made me do it." God looked at the serpent, the devil, and he said, "What can I say, I did it." (See Gen. 3:12–14.) So blame always goes back to the devil, "who made me do it." And now we have resolved the blame game!

The other thing about blame is that if we ever do decide who exactly was to blame, or what percentage of blame should be applied to each person, we're still left with the problem, the painful emotions, and what to do about it all. Empathy is the way out of the blame game.

3. "You're acting like a victim." Maybe when someone says this to us, we really are feeling like we have been victimized. The lack of empathy from the one we love does feel like cruel and unjust treatment. We usually act like a victim only when we feel in some way discounted. Sometimes we take on a long-standing victim position, but often that is not something we do all by ourselves. There is usually a "persecutor" in the mix who stirs within us a sense of helplessness, and then that fuels our feeling of being victimized. Sometimes we are victimized, but this statement is antithetical to empathy.

Action Plan #R9—Reverse Roles

Think back to the old days before you started to practice SMART Love. An argument would begin, and while one person was presenting their impassioned side of the argument, the other person would listen for a brief time to catch the flow of their argument and then stop listening. They already knew what their spouse was going to say. So instead of listening, they planned their rebuttal.

Of course, once the first spouse who seemingly started the argument stopped talking, the other spouse jumped in and presented their side. Then the first spouse repeated the pattern—they listened for a short time to catch the drift of the second person's argument, then stopped listening in order to restructure their point of view.

The point is, typically there are no surprises in these arguments. You both know what the other person is going to say. You really could argue either side of the issue. So here's the plan: Take an unfinished "argument" and switch sides. The husband has to argue the wife's point of view, and the wife has to argue the husband's point of view. Set a timer for ten minutes and see if you can last that long. When finished, laugh a bit at how each of you handled the opposite point of view, and then talk about what the other missed or overlooked in their presentation. Talk also about how well the other person captured your emotions as they presented your side of the argument.

Research has found that about two-thirds of the things couples argue about will never be resolved. Surprisingly, this statistic is the same for couples who are successful in their marriage and for couples who fail and end up divorced. The difference is that successful couples have learned how to dialogue about the problem and even eventually laugh together about "going around the same mountain again." Couples who fail in their marriage grow increasingly hostile as they hit the same roadblocks over and over again. Role reversal can help you learn to laugh together about the same old arguments.

Action Plan #R10—Get the Bigger Picture

One of the things I try to teach couples is that in their relationship, there is no such thing as absolute truth. All relational truth is subjective—it's how I see and experience something versus how you see and experience the same thing. It's like two people who have witnessed an accident from opposite corners of the street. What each saw was only part of the picture, and it was subjective based on their perspective. They may even offer conflicting accounts, because they saw what happened only from their individual vantage points. They both presented what they believed was the truth, but it was an incomplete truth, or what I call *subjective truth*.

It takes courage and strength to realize there is no point in arguing about subjective truth. The goal is to get the bigger picture, and like at an accident, that often requires an expansion of the subjective truth, or the acceptance that the "truth" is subjectively true. In the case of the accident scene, other factors will be brought in to come as close as possible to the absolute truth. There's the physical evidence, other eyewitness accounts, and the testimony of both drivers. Taken all together, a bigger picture is created, and it is usually closer to the reality of what happened.

Let's take it a step further. How about getting a bigger picture of how others see you? A close friend of mine invited six of us to a meeting in his conference room. He told us he wanted to get a more accurate picture of himself, so he was going to leave the room for an hour. The six of us were to come up with three characteristics that represented his strengths and as many characteristics as we wanted that represented his weaknesses. He encouraged us to be frank with him when he came back for our feedback.

That took courage on his part as well as ours. But we did what we were asked to do, and an hour later he returned. It was like asking six people to do a fearless moral inventory of him—I was glad it was him and not me. Yet it turned out to be an incredible experience for him as he invited the feedback so he could get a more accurate picture of himself. He wanted to get closer to the real truth about himself.

Don't be afraid of the bigger picture. Enlarge the picture!

12

T—Together in the Land of Emotions

Years ago, there was a cartoon in the Sunday comic section that I've always remembered. In the first box is a young couple, and the woman is asking the man, "How do you feel about that?" In the next box, he is stammering, "Uh, um, uh." Then in the third, bigger, full-color box, he is alone in a beautiful new place, asking, "Where am I?" In the final box, they are together again, and she is reassuring him, saying, "Relax, we're in the land of emotions!" And that's the goal of this last competency of SMART Love—to relax together in the land of emotions.

To get to this point together has meant we as a couple are motivated to grow. We have worked hard because we want to improve our fulfillment in our marriage. The Action Plans have called for taking the time to practice. And the more Action Plans we have successfully navigated, the more we have grown, both as an individual and as a couple. They have also required that we be open to feedback from our spouse. We need all three—motivation, practice, and feedback—to grow together emotionally in our relationship.

Let's imagine a wife who scored low on her ability to be empathic—to read her husband's emotions. It is hard for her to listen, for she believes she already knows what she needs to know. She interrupts her husband and doesn't pay close attention to what he is trying to tell her. For her to develop empathy and attunement, she needs to be motivated to change, practice listening to herself first, and then listen more carefully to her husband. She has to give up the idea that she can assume she knows what he is going to say, and that means she has to be willing to listen to feedback from her husband. They both have to recognize they are in this process together.

Or let's imagine a husband who can recognize his emotions only when he is angry, and he typically shows his anger by raising his voice and getting impatient. He has to face his basic fear about the strange world of the other emotions and feelings, be motivated to learn how to distinguish different feelings in himself, and be able to name them. For quite a while, he needs to carry around the word list of feelings and emotions until its contents become a part of him. He practices and practices until he becomes relaxed in the land of emotions. Obviously, to get to this point, he has learned a lot from the feedback given to him by his wife and friends.

When husbands and wives begin to relax together emotionally, they experience married life the way it was designed

169

to be. We aren't trying to create something unnatural—it's the norm, for we are wired to connect, and it is especially true that we are wired to connect emotionally. When we don't, something in us dies or goes into hiding. That's part of the design as well.

For example, when babies are born, they have over two hundred billion nerve cells, or neurons, in their brains. As adults, we end up with only one hundred billion nerve cells. What happened to the other one hundred billion? They died, and they were meant to die, because they did not connect with other cells. They were not used. Cells that fired together wired together, and they are the ones that survived. Everything about life is based on our cells wiring together, and our lives are meant to be wired together with significant others—to be connected to others. We don't survive in isolation.

The Problem of Balance

As we grow, life becomes more complex. In order for us to relax together emotionally, we have to be connected, and that means we have to resolve a basic personal contradiction. We must create a sense of resonance out of our personal dissonance. For the first months of a baby's life, he is working on one task—to be connected to Mom and to Dad. Eventually that comes into conflict with a countermove—the move to autonomy.

During "the terrible twos," the child is in a personal struggle between being connected and discovering some sense of autonomy. He wants to be connected to his mother and father. That's been his primary focus the first months of his life. But at some point, a conflicting drive kicked in and now he also wants to experience a sense of autonomy, which is the opposite of connection. One of his favorite sayings at this stage is "I can do it myself!" The other favorite is "no." About six months ago, my four-year-old granddaughter resolved this conflict for now. She's content again to be connected—she's had her first taste of independence, or autonomy, and it is basically at rest . . . until she becomes a teenager.

All this gets stirred up again during the teen years. Watch a teenager struggle with finding the balance, the resonance, between their drive to become an autonomous adult and still be a kid and part of the family. One minute they are arguing and angry, the next they are walking arm in arm with you, maybe even holding your hand. It's their attempt to find resonance between the drive for autonomy and the need to be connected.

To succeed in marriage requires that we resolve the same conflict. How can I be connected with my spouse and yet still be me? Prior to our getting married and continuing into the early stages of marriage, this isn't a problem. We are working on being connected and are willing to ignore our need to still be ourselves. But then at some point, we start to feel "too connected," as if we are losing ourselves.

We can picture the conflict as sometimes we are moving toward each other to connect, but at the same time we are moving away from each other to protect our autonomy. SMART Love represents the resolution in that we move to where we can be emotional with each other in a managed, empathic way, while at the same time we are more competent in our autonomy because we are comfortable in our emotions. We have together learned to relax in the land of emotions.

As we'll see, the results also include other skills, such as having the ability to communicate more clearly, quickly disarm potential conflict situations, and build stronger connections with each other and with other significant people in our lives. And we do these things with a higher degree of kindness and even humor.

Family Influences

Part of our ability to relax together emotionally is a resolution of the differing influences of our family of origin. As we were growing up, we were taught to follow the unique rules of our family, especially in the area of emotions. Different families allow for the expression of some emotions but not others. Some families allow only positive emotions: "If you're going to be sad (or mad), go to your room until you can put a smile on your face." Other families don't allow emotions, for everything is focused on performance. If you have an emotion, you just have to tough it out on your own. There are all kinds of family rules for every emotion and how they should and should not be expressed.

Researcher Paul Ekman talks about how our family of origin had what he calls "display rules."[1] Some families allow for the strong expression of all emotions, while others allow a strong expression of only certain emotions. Other families prefer a weak, quiet expression of emotions. The weak display might be experienced as talking quietly with Mom about what's bothering me. Add to the display rules the training we received in "being nice." We may have been told, "Go tell the lady you're sorry, and do it with a smile," when we were not sorry and we certainly didn't want to smile. But we learned to do it anyway.

Now think about the fact that no two people grow up the same way. Even siblings experience the family and its rules differently from each other. Therefore, you and your spouse came to your marriage with different family rules, and these rules needed to be negotiated early in the marriage. But typically they aren't negotiated; they're just there under the surface ready to frustrate us. That is, until you learn to love SMART. Now you have your own rules, and rule number one is to relax together emotionally.

Resonance

When we can relax together emotionally, we begin to experience a growing resonance with each other. One could say that our two egos are discovering there are actually times when they are in emotional harmony. That's called resonance. Its opposite, dissonance, is what we experience when our egos are not in harmony. But as we relax together emotionally, we can increase those times of resonance. We've discussed this in terms of the conflicting drives toward autonomy and the need for connection. These two drives are by nature dissonant, and maturity means working to make them harmonious with each other—that's resonance. I can be who I am and, at the same time, be connected to my spouse.

Now think of this desire for resonance in terms of just our gender differences. We joke a lot about how men will never stop to ask for directions unless it's a last resort. We joke because it is generally true, and it drives wives crazy. Or how men won't go see a doctor, even though their wives urge or even beg them to do so. I often point to these differences to prove that every marriage is an incompatible one, simply because of our gender differences.

Then add in our personality differences, which at first attracted us to each other but later become unacceptable. They quickly became the agenda for change—the other person must become a clone of me. And when we include the differing family backgrounds, it's easy to understand why we experience a lot of dissonance and very little resonance. As we become more competent at SMART Love, we gradually overcome the dissonance and restore resonance—the harmony of two hearts beating as one.

This is hard work. We knew before that it's only in fairy tales that the story ends with the words, "They lived happily ever after." But we all have had the dream of living happily ever after. We know all too well that in real life, happily ever after runs head-on into life's ups and downs. That's why we need to learn the art of married life. It requires work to create harmony, but it is worth the effort!

Contagious Emotions

Our emotions are like a contagious infection. Hang around someone else for a while, and you'll catch the same emotion they have. That's why the negative emotions are so destructive to harmony. They are caught by the other person. Remember the story of Don and Pat. Pat started from the basic emotional posture of fear. But as Don ramped up his basic emotional posture of anger, her fears quickly changed into her own expression of anger. Don's anger was contagious, and Pat quickly caught the disease. The more upset one person becomes, the more the other person synchronizes what they feel with what the upset person feels.

What's true of the negative core emotions is even more true when you look at the contagion of the positive emotions. Let's say the husband has had a good day at the office and comes home all hyped up about what happened. If a couple has learned to relax emotionally, the wife will soon be in harmony with his up mood. Even if she's had a bad day, her need to talk about her day with her husband may dissipate as she is able to enter into his up mood. It lifts her emotionally to where they are in harmony. In fact, his up mood may even calm her and enable her to lift herself out of her down mood.

This is, of course, based on the authenticity of the emotions, feelings, and moods. You can't fake it, as it will be obvious to your spouse. We're talking about the contagiousness of authentic emotions and feelings. If one person pretends to feel something, like being happy, the other spouse quickly picks up on the fact that it is not authentic. They may not pick up on the "emotion," but they do pick up on the lack of authenticity in it. Any faked emotion will quickly be seen as such and will not be contagious.

The Evidence of Harmony

Now that you have worked at becoming more competent in using all the skills of SMART Love, here is a review of some of the great things you will experience together. You will have found that your communication skills have grown. You were once misunderstood perhaps because you didn't know what you were feeling, or maybe you were afraid to say what you meant. Now you are increasingly able to talk to each other in a clear and direct way that is seldom misunderstood. Not only is this true in your marriage relationship, but it also shows itself in how you more clearly communicate with your kids, your extended family, and your friends and co-workers.

Your social skills in general have improved. Since you have learned to monitor and manage your own emotions, you are better able to anticipate the reactions of others. You are also more able to fine-tune your own social abilities to where you can make a good and authentic impression on other people.

You have become more capable in your ability to negotiate with each other. Shouting matches and hurt feelings from being misunderstood are now rare occurrences. You are able to resolve some of the recalcitrant issues. It has always amazed me how people can be highly competent at negotiation in the workplace, but they seldom think about bringing those skills home. It seems to me that it's equally or even more important to be able to negotiate a situation with our spouse and family than it is to negotiate something successfully at work.

When it comes to making changes together, it no longer stirs up resistance and fear. You no longer just go along to get along. You are open to new ideas and are willing to discuss the possibility and the need for change. As part of this openness, you are willing to receive feedback from each other and even from your family. Your desire is to learn and to become more competent emotionally. Now, instead of one of you getting defensive when your spouse offers feedback, you see it as a means to grow and gain self-knowledge.

An important bonus is that you are better able, as a couple and in your family, to manage your potential conflicts. It's not that conflicts don't exist—the potential will be there as long as two separate and different people are living together and are invested in the relationship. But now these situations seldom get out of control, for you both have learned how to better manage your own emotions as well as manage the conflict. What a relief!

Finally, you increasingly find that you are able to work more together as a team. You actually feel like you *are* a team. Before, it felt like you were often standing face-to-face, struggling to work things out. Now it feels like you are standing side by side, looking forward and working together. You are a team with a purpose—to move your marriage in the right direction. You are seeking to build a meaningful, fulfilling, and satisfying relationship that will be a model of success for others and will be enjoyed by each of you. You can relax together in the land of emotions!

Now let's work on some Action Plans that will help us relax more with all we've learned.

Together Emotionally
Action Plans

So far, we've worked on competency in the personal skills of becoming more self-aware, especially of our emotions. We worked on being able to manage our emotions. Then we worked on the joint skills related to being accountable as a couple, and finally on being empathic, especially with our spouse. Now we put it all together and look at the skills of being relaxed together with our emotions as we effectively manage our marital and family relationships.

A great marriage doesn't just happen. It takes work. But fortunately, our brains cooperate in that when we do the work, the comfort and bonding hormones of dopamine and oxytocin are released. Even with that, a great marriage takes effort and practice. Aging and maturity, by themselves, are not enough.

Hopefully you have worked through a number of the Action Plans for each competency area. Don't let up now. Here are ten more Action Plans designed to strengthen your relationship together. They are based on your growing competencies with the other four sets of Action Plans, and these are designed to be experienced together.

Action Plan #T1—Try an Experiment in Resonance

This is an experiment designed for the two of you to experience resonance together. Find a quiet, comfortable spot, free from distractions. Set aside fifteen to twenty minutes when you won't be disturbed. You may even want to take the phone off the hook and turn off your cell phones for that length of time.

Make certain you both are in a good mood. Sit so you can hold one of your spouse's hands and look into each other's eyes. Take some deep breaths and sit there quietly, looking into each other's eyes, smiling at each other, and holding hands. Sit like this silently for fifteen minutes.

At the end of fifteen minutes, notice how you are breathing. Then take your pulse. What typically happens is that at the end of fifteen minutes, your heart rates will synchronize. They should beat together and be in the same range of beats per minute. For this to work, your smile needs to be authentic, as does the level of comfort you feel with each other. You've just experienced resonance!

Action Plan #T2—Give and Accept Feedback

Feedback is much easier to give than to receive. But the gifts of feedback are in the receiving. When a couple is able to give each other both positive and negative feedback, they are in a solid growth pattern. But giving feedback to a spouse can be a dangerous undertaking, especially when it is uninvited. And even when it is invited, it still can be difficult to hear. It easily can feel like criticism.

Here are some guidelines on how to receive invited feedback. First, you must sincerely give each other permission to share it. Remind yourself that you have given your spouse permission to give you this feedback.

Second, consider the source of the feedback. It's coming from your spouse, who loves you. Remind yourself that it's being offered in love. Slow down, take a deep breath, and listen.

Third, simply listen to what is being said to you. Do not evaluate whether you agree or disagree with it. Don't argue, attempt to explain, or try to defend yourself. Just listen and take it in. Take some time to consider the truth in your spouse's words. Because they are being said by someone who loves you and cares about you, you can assume the feedback is in your best interest.

Fourth, when the feedback is complete, talk together and decide what needs to be done with the information. Then make a commitment to implement any change you have agreed to.

Keep these four points in mind as, with permission, you give feedback to your spouse. Remind yourself that it is to be given in love. Think also about the fact that it is probably as hard for your spouse to receive feedback as it was for you. So couch your feedback with a degree of tentativeness, while at the same time not diluting what you are saying.

Work together on how to implement what is being considered. When you are truly relaxed together in the world of emotions, this will become more natural and less threatening for you both.

Action Plan #T3—Have That Tough Conversation You've Been Avoiding

Most couples have hidden somewhere a tough conversation that they keep shifting to a back burner, hoping the issue will resolve itself. It is usually loaded with potential negative emotions, and unfortunately, it is resilient—it just won't go away. Set a time when you will face the issue together. Here's a plan for how to have that conversation you've been avoiding.

First, begin with some part of the issue upon which you can agree. It may be some facet of the issue, or it may simply be the fact that you both want to put the issue to rest. If you're the one starting the conversation, point out the focus of agreement as a starting point for the conversation. Then carefully state the subject.

Second, ask your spouse to review the background information on the issue from their point of view. You are basically asking them to help you better understand how they see the problem. What's the point of their side of the issue? Listening again to your spouse's point of view shows you care and are interested in knowing more about how they feel, even though you may have already been through this several times before.

Third, when your spouse is giving their perspective on the problem, listen. Do not counter with your point of view, nor should you try to explain anything that you disagree with or feel they are overlooking. At this stage, you simply listen.

Fourth, when your spouse is finished, it's your turn to give your side of the issue. Your spouse is to listen the same way you did, without defending or explaining or attempting to counter your argument. Try to help your spouse understand how you see things. Since both of you have developed your emotional self-awareness and the ability to manage what you are feeling, you should be able to communicate clearly and simply without getting defensive or overly emotional.

Finally, after you have each expressed your side of the issue, enter into a brief discussion to see if there is anything new that can help put to rest at least part of the subject. Discuss what both of you should do next. You want to avoid an endless circular argument that simply rehashes everything you've already said.

Some problems are never fully resolved, and this may be one of them. If so, it helps to have a dialogue together about the problem, and to find some humor in an "Are we going to go around that mountain again?" approach. At worst, you are able to comfortably disagree while staying connected. At best, you get new insight into how the issue may be resolved.

Action Plan #T4—Understand Your Different Communication Styles

We've found in working with couples that there are two basic, and opposite, communication styles we bring to a marriage.

The Literal Style of Communication

1. You are a person who tries to live passionately in today.
2. You like detail.

3. You work things through in a linear pattern of thought.

4. You like going step-by-step.

5. You say what you mean and mean what you say.

6. You tend to speak with complete thoughts.

7. When you leave your spouse a note, it has complete sentences with a period at the end of each.

The Inferential Style of Communication

1. You typically love to live in the future.

2. Tomorrow is your favorite day of the week.

3. You talk a lot about your goals.

4. You are more global in your gathering of information.

5. You say less than what you mean and assume the listener can fill in the rest.

6. You speak and write with incomplete thoughts.

7. You leave a note for your spouse with a few words and a dash. You don't leave things out because you are malicious; you simply don't have words yet for what's left out.

People are often attracted, for some reason, to their opposite. Then the differences are complicated by the fact that we listen the same way we talk. A literal communicator listens to others and assumes they are being literal. It's like they erase the dash of the inferential communicator, who only said part of what they meant, and replace it with a period. Then they have a habit of saying, "But you said . . ." as they try to hold the inferential communicator to a literal interpretation of what was said.

The inferential communicator does the same thing, only from the opposite position. They listen and assume the literal speaker is communicating inferentially. They firmly believe there is always more than what is being said. They erase the literal communicator's period and replace it with a dash, assuming they can read the other's mind and know what they meant to say. But of course, the literal communicator said all they meant to say the first time.

Here's an example: A literal communicator asks his inferential wife if she wants to go out to eat tonight. She says no. The literal communicator assumes she meant no and goes to the family room to start doing something else. Then he hears the pans banging and the cupboard doors slamming, so he goes back into the kitchen and asks, "What's wrong?"

She answers, "I guess I wanted to go out to eat tonight."

"But you said 'No' when I asked you."

"Yes," she replies, "but you should always know that when I say 'No,' I mean 'No, but . . .'"

"No, but what?" the literal communicator responds. And then the inferential communicator lists a number of concerns that were unstated. Since she was at first frustrated at being taken at her word and her spouse continued the conversation, she is now able to access the rest of what she wanted to communicate.

When she finishes, her husband asks, "Why couldn't you just say that when I asked if you wanted to go out to eat?"

And her sincere reply is, "I didn't know all of that until you took me at my word."

For the literal communicator to get at what the inferential communicator is unaware of not being able to say, he could have paraphrased the "no." An effective reply to the "no" would have been, "Really, you don't want to go out to eat?" And that would release more of the inferential person's message, at least one part at a time. Both should clarify important communication by paraphrasing what they just heard. This will help the inferential listener to pare down their assumptions about their spouse, and it will help the literal listener expand the inferential response of their spouse.

We've found these differences to be very common in couples. And they lead to misunderstandings. A lot of frustration can be overcome when a person finally feels like they are being heard by their spouse. Taking the time to paraphrase what was just heard is like magically opening a door to understanding.

Keep in mind that both communication styles are legitimate ways of organizing information and communicating. Both are right and neither is wrong.

Action Plan #T5—Show Appreciation

Sometimes showing appreciation takes more than a simple "thanks." It takes some thought. There are times when a spouse goes the extra mile in covering for us, or in supporting us when we are under pressure. We may be under the gun at work, or our leadership in some charitable event is in jeopardy, or our kids have created a mess that had to be undone, and our spouse has willingly picked up the slack for us.

When this happens, take some time to think through what would be a special way to say more than "thanks." It may be a special dinner, or it may simply be a handwritten card that expresses a genuine appreciation for what was done. Basically, your appreciation of the extra effort of your spouse should not go unnoticed—there are meaningful ways that communicate more than a casual thank-you, and a special thanks makes a positive impact that strengthens the marriage relationship.

Action Plan #T6—Create a Marriage Mission Statement

Successful businesses today all have a mission statement. It explains in a short sentence why a business is in business. Our church has a mission statement, which says that we are "following Jesus Christ to lead lives that reveal God's goodness." When someone reads that mission statement, they know some important things about our church.

Some years ago, the two of us spent a weekend in the mountains with the purpose of working on a mission statement as a couple. For part of the exercise, we asked ourselves, "What would we want on our tombstones?" We spent most of a day sitting by a running creek in the woods, talking about what we thought our mission in life was as a couple.

The result: our mission statement is "to be facilitators of healing in people's relationships." One of our sons has as his mission statement "to provide a stable home for our children." We designed our statement to fit a lot of what we were already doing. That statement applied to Dave's focus as a therapist. It fit what we attempted to do together in our seminars, and it described what we attempt to do in writing books and in doing *New Life Live* radio and TV. Over the years, we have evaluated opportunities in light of our mission statement and turned some things down because they didn't fit our mission. It's part of our working together as a team—deciding what we say yes to and what we say no to.

Spend a day in the mountains by a running stream or at some other favorite spot and work out how you want to be known as a couple. What's your purpose? How do you want to be remembered? Write it out and keep it in focus as you make decisions and evaluate what you are to do in the future.

Action Plan #T7—Avoid Giving Mixed Signals

It's easy to give our spouse and other family members mixed signals. Let's say that something happened at work that really triggered anger in you, but you couldn't deal with it at the time. You had to push it aside and act as if nothing was wrong. Then at home that evening, something your spouse says hooks right into that anger. You are aware of the anger and are able to a degree to manage it, but it shows in your body language, your tone of voice, and your ability to communicate. You've just given out mixed signals.

The same thing can happen when you come home and right away you know that your wife has had a very bad day. She lets you know that she has been dealing with your two-year-old son and nothing is going right between them. And then you as the dad walk in the door all frustrated by something that happened at work. You try to set aside your issues temporarily, but the frustration leaks through in your difficulty in listening to your wife. Then she thinks you don't care about her stressful day.

Managing our marital relationship requires that we first become aware of how we inadvertently mix our signals, and then avoid mixing the messages we are giving out verbally and nonverbally. The best path is to acknowledge the struggle you are having with your day, and say something like, "I'm sorry. I had a bad experience today and I'm very distracted. Give me a minute to get myself in sync and then let's talk."

Pay close attention to how your unacknowledged emotions can confuse your verbal and nonverbal signals. A simple example is that you tell your spouse you are doing fine when you are not. Be honest about where you are emotionally. Agree to give each other loving feedback when the signals are mixed.

Action Plan #T8—Make a Plan for Using Anger

Healthy anger typically has a purpose. It can be constructive, like when a coach gets riled up about how his team is playing and gives an impassioned speech at halftime. But it can also be unhealthy and become destructive when it is out of control. It is also unhealthy when it represents holding on to something that happened in the past and takes the form of bitterness or resentment.

Remember, the apostle Paul tells us, "Don't sin by letting anger control you" (Eph. 4:26). And Aristotle urged us to be angry, but to "be angry with the right person, to the right degree, at the right time, for the right purpose, and in the right way."[1] So let's take each of the expressions of anger and discuss how to manage the anger properly and, if necessary, use it for the right purpose.

Relationally, anger is probably the hardest emotion to manage, and it can definitely be the most hurtful and destructive emotion in any relationship. So in order to relax emotionally with each other, let's put some extra effort into better understanding how each of us behaves in the presence of the feelings related to anger. You've already worked on being able to manage the emotion of anger back in chapters 7 and 8. But now let's take it a step further and work on how we can better manage the emotion and feelings of anger together.

First, talk together about the common ways you each experience and express the emotion of anger. For example, what makes you touchy? What makes you frustrated? What makes you furious? Go through the list below and identify which feelings tend to trip you up. Discuss how your expression of each feeling is used the wrong way, at the wrong time, to the wrong degree, or for the wrong purpose. In what ways is its expression hurtful? Talk about possible ways a different expression of anger could actually be helpful.

Explain why you think these are your typical responses and what types of situations trigger each of your typical feelings related to anger. Remember, managing together your shared emotional worlds is what this competency is about.

You may want to make some notes below next to your more common expressions of anger.

The Expression	When Does It Happen?	What Are the Triggers?
Furious		
Enraged		
Irate		
Seething		
Upset		
Frustrated		
Annoyed		
Irritated		
Touchy		

It's important that you be honest not only with yourself but also with each other. Talking about the behavioral expressions of various levels of anger is important if your goal is to be relaxed together in the world of emotions.

Action Plan #T9—Be Curious about Your Spouse

I never stop being amazed at people who have no clue why their spouse feels a certain way about a situation. When I ask them if they know why their spouse feels as they do, and their answer is no, my next question is, "Aren't you curious about why they feel as they do?" I may get either a yes or a no answer, but then when I ask what, to me, is the next logical question— "Why don't you ask them now?"—I often encounter a passive resistance. It seems to me like they really don't want to know.

Maybe it's simply a part of my training as a therapist, but I'm always curious. I can drive my wife crazy sometimes with wanting to know more. I've practiced a lot with how to ask questions, both at home and at my office. Sometimes it's appropriate to be curious about what our mate is thinking or feeling.

Curiosity means you ask each other questions. It also means you have developed some skill in how to ask them. Questions are not designed to put your spouse under pressure or to seek sensitive information. Their purpose is to increase your understanding of your spouse and your knowledge of them at a deeper level.

It's also important to follow up your questions with discussion. Continuing the search for better understanding with added conversation will show you are genuinely interested in what is being said. Curiosity can lead not only to better understanding but also to a greater degree of openness between you and your spouse.

Action Plan #T10—Practice Courtesy

One of the important things that tends to fade away in many marriages is a simple thing like courtesy. How long has it been since you said "thank you" to your spouse? When was the last time you put "please" in your request? And here's the one that really gets to me: how long has it been since you've heard "I'm sorry"? I've worked with many couples where one of them will tell me, "I don't think my spouse has ever said 'I'm sorry' in our marriage!" How can that be? No one's perfect, so there must always be an appropriate "I'm sorry" in a relationship. The one who never says that is disconnected from their spouse.

If you don't use these phrases very often, you may simply be out of practice. So to begin practicing with your spouse, find three things every day for which you can say "thank you," and three things for which you can say "please." Don't limit your practicing to your spouse. Throughout your activities on any day, find situations where you can purposely and appropriately say "please" and "thank you."

When it comes to saying "I'm sorry," you may need some help getting started. Ask your spouse for examples of situations that still need an apology. Don't get defensive and don't explain—simply listen and then sincerely say "I'm sorry." You may be amazed at the warm response you will get to a sincere "I'm sorry"!

Remember that many of the Action Plans are exercises in the behaviors of love. As you and your spouse develop the competencies of SMART Love, you will at the same time be deepening your love for each other. Let's look now at how love fits into the whole picture.

14

What about Love?

We might think that love would be listed as one of the basic emotions. After all, it's what we strive for and what we will even die for. It's what led us to get married, and it's what's supposed to make the world go round. But in all the literature related to EQ and business, love is never included in the discussion.

Yet we agree that it is complex. Look at the definition of love given by Wikipedia:

> Love is a variety of different feelings, states, and attitudes that ranges from interpersonal affection ("I love my mother") to pleasure ("I loved that meal"). It can refer to an emotion of a strong attraction and personal attachment. It can also be a virtue representing human kindness, compassion, and affection. . . . It may also describe compassionate and affectionate actions towards other humans, one's self, or animals.[1]

That covers a lot of territory.

In the English language, we have only one word for *love*, and it applies to all the various ways it is used. The ancient Greeks had five words for *love*. *Agape* is a New Testament word that describes an unconditional form of love that expects nothing in return: "I will *agape* you no matter what." *Phileo*, also a word used in the New Testament, describes a brotherly type of love, hence the name of the city of brotherly love—Philadelphia. *Eros* refers to a sexual kind of love, and we get the word *erotic* from it. *Storge* describes the kind of love a child has for their parent. *Xenia* describes love as hospitality.

What Is Love?

Robert Sternberg, a Yale University psychologist, defines what he calls the "mystery of love." He says, "Love is one of the most intense and desirable of human emotions. People may lie, cheat, steal, and even kill in its name—and wish to die when they lose it. Love can overwhelm anyone at any age."[2]

One of our favorite definitions of love is "an emotional, volitional response to an intellectual evaluation of another person." We used that definition while teaching a college Sunday school class years ago. After the class a young man came up to us and said, "I like that definition. I've been dating several girls, and I think it's time I get married. So I'm going to make an intellectual evaluation of them and then decide who I'm going to marry."

We weren't sure we wanted to have that definition taken so seriously and so quickly. But the next week he introduced us to Linda, his future bride. Later we asked him how he had decided. He said he had made a list of all the positive things he liked about each of the girls he was dating. Then he wrote out what he thought might be the problems they would face as a couple. After letting what he had written sit for a while, he went back to it to see what his emotional response was. Linda was the clear winner according to his heart's response. They married, and he went on to seminary and became a pastor. Last I heard, he was enjoying a good relationship with Linda, who, when we asked her, said she knew how he had decided.

C. S. Lewis described love this way: "Love, in the Christian sense, does not mean an emotion. It is a state not of the feelings but of the will; that state of the will which we have naturally about ourselves, and must learn to have about other people."[3] This Christian contribution to the understanding of love is not only recognized by Robert Sternberg but incorporated into his definition of love. His research on love led him to develop a three-part definition consisting of intimacy, passion, and commitment. He called it the triangle of love.

Intimacy can be described as the emotions we have that make us feel close to our spouse—connected and bonded to each other. It includes liking each other and knowing each other deeply. Obviously, to do this, we have to communicate with each other—a behavior.

Passion almost automatically takes us to the physical and sexual aspects of marriage. In King Solomon's Song of Songs, the woman described passion at its most ardent level in this way: "For love is as strong as death, its jealousy as enduring as the grave. Love flashes like fire, the brightest kind of flame" (Song of Songs 8:6). But passion goes beyond just the physical. It involves the excitement we have at just being together, the sense of well-being we have doing just about anything together.

It is interesting that Sternberg's first two components of love involve both decision and emotion. Intimacy takes place when we first decide to spend time opening up to our spouse, and then its feelings follow. Passion begins as an emotion, then is kept alive by making ongoing behavioral decisions to continue to enjoy our spouse. *Commitment* is basically a decision; it doesn't have the emotion that intimacy and passion have. However, it is an equally important piece in understanding love.

There are basically two decisions involved with commitment. First is the decision to love—to make the initial commitment. This is a clearly defined decision. But it is followed by an equally important ongoing decision we make regularly—to maintain and nurture that first decision to love and to grow our love. Those two decisions get us through the crisis times every couple will experience at some point in time. They also get us through those inevitable times when the feelings of love are weak or even absent. And those decisions are especially important when loving the other isn't easy.

The Behaviors of Love

Psychologist Erich Fromm, in his book *The Art of Loving*, made the point that love is more than a feeling or an emotion; it also includes behavior. He says that the feelings of love are secondary when compared to the behaviors of love. This wasn't something new, for the apostle Paul, when he wrote the "love chapter" (1 Cor. 13), did not make a single reference to an emotion or a feeling. It is all about the behaviors of love. Fromm points out that some people have tried to study love and end up saying it is just a glob of intense emotional experiences that cannot be understood. Others have tried to break it down into so many pieces that they end up explaining nothing.

Paul begins the love chapter by noting the importance of being loving: "If I could speak all the languages of earth and of angels, but didn't love others, I would only be a noisy gong or a clanging cymbal" (v. 1). He adds that without love, we end up being nothing. In verses 4–7, he gives us a list of behaviors of love that make up his definition of it:

> Love is patient and kind. Love is not jealous or boastful or proud or rude. It does not demand its own way. It is not irritable, and it keeps no record of being wronged. It does not rejoice about injustice but rejoices whenever the truth wins out. Love never gives up, never loses faith, is always hopeful, and endures through every circumstance.

Not a feeling or an emotion in the list! Love, to Paul, is all about behavior.

I've found in working with couples that when the behaviors of love begin to wear thin, the feelings of love also begin to wane. When the behaviors of love are restored, the feelings of love return. That's why the feelings of love are secondary to the behaviors of love in a marriage. Show each other the behaviors of love, and the feelings of love will be there.

That also explains why Jesus, in talking with his disciples, could command that they love one another. How do you command an emotion? You can't. It's not like you can turn on an emotion by decree. But he told them, "This is my commandment: Love each other in the same way I have loved you" (John 15:12). Then he went on to describe how he loved the disciples: "There is no greater love than to lay down one's life for one's friends" (v. 13). That's love expressed as a behavior. And soon Jesus would demonstrate his love through his behavior by becoming the sacrifice for our sins on the cross.

SMART Love, as many of the Action Plans in this book will show, is based on doing the behaviors of love, particularly as those behaviors relate to the area of our emotions. Our goal has been to increase our emotional knowledge. If we can identify our emotions, manage them, be accountable to each other, and show empathy to each other, these behaviors of love *will* create the strong feelings of love we so desire.

Here's a suggested exercise. When one of our founding fathers, Ben Franklin, was twenty years old, he wanted to make certain he cultivated the development of his character. He created a list of thirteen virtues, defined them, and then determined to practice each one for a week. In three months he would work his way through the list and then start over. As a printer, he was able to create a small booklet to track his progress. On the left-hand page he described one of the virtues, and on the right-hand page he made a weekly chart. At the end of each day, he would mark with a black dot on a graph that showed whether he had succeeded or failed in living up to that virtue.

What if we did something similar? Below is the list of the apostle Paul's fifteen behaviors of love, taken from the New International Version. Begin with "love is patient," and talk with your spouse about how you define patience and areas of your lives where patience is difficult. Then work on being patient with each other for a week. During that time, mention the positive examples of when you each have been patient with the other. The next week, work on "love is kind," and so on, working your way through the list of behaviors.

Love:
1. Is patient
2. Is kind
3. Does not envy
4. Does not boast
5. Is not proud
6. Does not dishonor others
7. Is not self-seeking
8. Is not easily angered
9. Keeps no record of wrongs
10. Does not delight in evil
11. Rejoices with the truth
12. Always protects
13. Always trusts
14. Always hopes
15. Always perseveres

Doing this exercise guarantees strengthening your ability to love each other and to recognize the uniqueness of what we call love. Deepening our love for each other is the goal of SMART Love and the primary outcome of our developing its five skills.

Love Is Unique

There are other ways that the emotion of love is unique. Consider this: each of the basic emotions we've discussed has a purpose. There is something we are called to do once we have experienced that emotion in a healthy way. Then, once we do whatever that is, we are supposed to stop experiencing the emotion. It has served its purpose. For example, our amygdala warns us of impending danger so we will experience either anger or fear. We experience one of those to motivate us to take action and protect ourselves. We will do this through fighting, taking flight, or freezing in place. Once we have protected ourselves, the emotion dissipates, for it has served its purpose. Similarly, the healthy expression of sadness has the purpose of enabling us to grieve a loss. In the same way, shame's purpose is to motivate us to make things right.

This, of course, is only true when the emotion is being expressed in a healthy way—in the here and now. In its unhealthy form, we get stuck in an emotion and it becomes our basic emotional posture (BEP), whether that's fear, anger, toxic shame, or depression. These four emotions are not meant to linger, only to come when needed and then go. It's when they linger that they become unhealthy.

On the contrary, love is meant to be a steadfast experience. In its healthy form, it's meant to come, to stay, and to grow stronger over the years. It doesn't basically increase or decrease in response to the changing environment or the changing circumstances or needs of the lover. Real love, therefore, is in a category of its own! The truth about love is that it is a constant. We didn't "fall in love" in order to "fall out of love." When we love, our intention is to stay in love.

Our hope in writing this book is to launch you on a journey of love that leads you to enjoy visiting the land of emotions safely. But it is a journey of many steps, which means it will take time and energy to work through the Action Plans for each competency. We invite you to come back again and again to the Action Plans in order to become ever more competent in each facet of SMART Love. It's not an easy journey, for you will be taking risks each step of the way. But if at times you think of giving up the journey, ponder these words from C. S. Lewis:

> To love at all is to be vulnerable. Love anything, and your heart will certainly be wrung and possibly be broken. If you want to make sure of keeping it intact, you must give your heart to no one, not even to an animal. Wrap it carefully round with hobbies and little luxuries; avoid all entanglements; lock it up safe in the casket or coffin of your selfishness. But in that casket—safe, dark, motionless, airless—it will change. It will not be broken; it will become unbreakable, impenetrable, irredeemable. The only place outside Heaven where you can be perfectly safe from all the dangers and perturbations of love is Hell.[4]

Love is everywhere. It's in a hug with your spouse, a special touch on the arm, the concern of a friend, and even the look your pet gives you. You can be mad at the person you love, but you still love them. You can even be disappointed in them, but love remains. Love goes far deeper and lasts far longer than any of the emotions we've worked with in this book. So love stands on its own, and that's why we call it SMART Love!

NOTES

Introduction

1. Travis Bradberry and Jean Greaves, *Emotional Intelligence 2.0* (San Diego: TalentSmart, 2009), 14.

Chapter 1 What Is SMART Love?

1. Aristotle, *The Nicomachean Ethics* (New York: Oxford University Press, 2009).

Chapter 2 The Land of Emotions

1. Paul Ekman, *Emotions Revealed* (New York: Owl Books, 2007).

Chapter 4 S—Self-Awareness

1. William Styron, *Darkness Visible: A Memoir of Madness* (New York: Vantage Books, 1990), 64.

Chapter 5 Self-Awareness Action Plans

1. Barry Lopez, *Arctic Dreams* (New York: Bantam Books, 1987), 97–98.

Chapter 6 M—Managing Your Emotions

1. To better understand this, see David Stoop, *You Are What You Think* (Grand Rapids: Revell, 2003).

Chapter 11 Empathy Action Plans

1. Pat Conroy, *The Prince of Tides* (Boston: Houghton Mifflin, 1986), 7.

2. For more on this subject, see David Stoop, *You Are What You Think* (Grand Rapids: Revell, 2003).

Chapter 12 *T*—Together in the Land of Emotions

1. Ekman, *Emotions Revealed*, xx.

Chapter 13 Together Emotionally Action Plans

1. Aristotle, *The Nicomachean Ethics.*

Chapter 14 What about Love?

1. *Wikipedia*, s.v. "Love," last modified March 18, 2016, https://en.wikipedia.org/wiki/Love.

2. Robert J. Sternberg, *The Triangle of Love: Intimacy, Passion, Commitment* (New York: Basic Books, 1980), 284.

3. C. S. Lewis, *Mere Christianity* (New York: Macmillan, 1952), 113.

4. C. S. Lewis, *The Four Loves* (New York: Harcourt Brace Jovanovich, 1960), 169.

Dr. **David Stoop** is a licensed clinical psychologist and the founder and director of the Center for Family Therapy. He is the author of more than thirty books, including *Forgiving What You'll Never Forget* and *Rethink How You Think*. He is a graduate of Fuller Theological Seminary, where he is also an adjunct professor, and received his doctorate from the University of Southern California. He is frequently heard as a cohost on the nationally syndicated *New Life Live!* radio and TV program.

Dr. **Jan Stoop** is a graduate of Fuller Theological Seminary and received her doctorate in psychology from the California Graduate Institute. She has coauthored books with her husband, and together they have led seminars and retreats worldwide on marital relationships and forgiveness. They have three sons and six wonderful grandchildren.

Learn more at www.drstoop.com.